Think Like a Test Maker

Teacher Certification Exam Test Prep

ESOL/ESL

How to pass any ESOL/ESL teacher certification exam using proven strategies, relevant content, and applicable practice test questions.

By: Kathleen Jasper, Ed.D.

Kathleen Jasper

Kathleen Jasper LLC
Estero, FL 33928
http://www.kathleenjasper.com | info@KathleenJasper.com

Think Like a Test Maker **ESOL/ESL Teacher Certification Exam Test Prep:** How to pass any ESOL/ESL teacher certification exam using proven strategies, relevant content, and applicable practice test questions.

Printed in the United States of America
ISBN: 9798753795410

Thank you for taking the time to purchase this book. I really appreciate it.

Would you mind leaving a review?

Did you purchase this book on Amazon? If so, I would be thrilled if you would leave an unbiased review at your convenience. Did you purchase this book from KathleenJasper.com? If so, you can leave a review on Facebook, Google, or directly on our website on the product page. Thank you for using my products.

Visit my Facebook Page.

I post videos, practice test questions, upcoming events, and other resources daily on my Facebook Page. Join us every Tuesday at 5 P.M. ET for our Facebook live math help session.

https://www.facebook.com/KathleenJasperEdD.

Check out my other products.

I have built several comprehensive, self-paced online courses for many teacher certification exams. I also have other books, webinars and more. Go to https://kathleenjasper.com and use offer code **ESOL20** for 20% off any of my products.

Join my private Facebook group.

Are you trying to become a teacher and looking for a community? Share insights, strategies and connect with other prospective teachers by joining my teacher certification Facebook group.

Go to: www.facebook.com/groups/certificationprep/ to request access.

Subscribe to my YouTube channel

Check out my enormous video library with tons of interesting and insightful content for teacher certification exams and more.

Subscribe here: https://www.youtube.com/kathleenjasperedd

If you have any questions, don't hesitate to reach out. It will be my pleasure to help.
Good luck on your exam.

–Kathleen Jasper, Ed.D.

This page intentionally left blank.

Table of Contents

A Note from the Author

I wrote this study guide using the test blueprints and specifications of several exams. The content and questions in this book are aligned to those blueprints and test specifications. I did this so you would be able to use this study guide for any state in which you are seeking certification.

It is important to understand that no matter what study guide you use, you will never see exact questions from the guide on your exam. The teacher certification exams are standardized assessments with large item banks. There is no way to know what form or what questions you will receive on test day. That is part of standard test security. That is why it is very important to understand the skills and content as well as the test questions. Simply doing practice tests over and over again will not prepare you adequately for this exam. You must work on acquiring the knowledge and skills outlined in the content sections of the book.

I recommend using this study guide in tandem with your state's blueprint and test specification along with the blueprints and test specifications I used to make this study guide. The following are the tests and links to the blueprints I used to inform the construction of this study guide:

Praxis English to Speakers of other Languages 5362

https://www.ets.org/s/praxis/pdf/5362.pdf

English as a Second Language Supplemental (154)

https://www.tx.nesinc.com/Content/StudyGuide/TX_SG_obj_154.htm

English as a Second Language

https://www.mtel.nesinc.com/Content/StudyGuide/MA_SG_OBJ_54.htm

Finally, I recommend watching this video on test administration. Understanding how to ***think like a test maker*** is a big part of passing your exam.

https://youtu.be/c92TPxR_m7w

With the right preparation and dedication, you can pass this test.

I believe in you,

Kathleen Jasper

Kathleen Jasper, Ed.D.

How to Use this Book

Often people will purchase a study guide and become overwhelmed with the amount of information and tasks within the guide. Below is a suggested way to use the book.

Step 1: Use the practice test at the end of the guide as a pretest. Do this first to measure your skills. This will be a baseline score.

- Take the practice test.

- Mark the ones you get incorrect, but DO NOT look at the correct answers or explanations. That way you can reuse this test later.

- Record your score. This will be your raw score out of 120 because there are 120 questions on the practice tests (Selected Response).

- Determine the categories and areas in which you are low.

Step 2: Begin your studies with your strengths and weaknesses in mind.

- Start with Category I.

- Read the information under each section. That information is very important.

- Work through all the information in the sections in the guide.

- Complete the 10 practice problems at the end of each content category. If you get less than 80% correct, go back through and review content category.

- Do this for all sections of the book.

Step 3: Once you've worked through the entire guide, take the practice test again.

- Work backwards starting with the answer choices first. Eliminate bad words, focus on good words. Then read the question stem.

- Check your answers and read ALL the answer explanations. There is a ton of information in the answer explanations, so even if you get the answer correct, read the explanation.

- Review information as needed.

- Take the second practice test. A score of 80% or higher means you are ready to take the real exam.

Step 4: Practice the constructed response portion of the exam.

- Whether you have writing on your test or not, this practice will help you, so I recommend working through it.

QUICK TIPS: These tips are represented with a megaphone and include tips and vocabulary you need to know or strategies for answering questions for a particular skill or content category.

 THINK LIKE A TEST MAKER: These tips are represented with a light bulb and are specific test taking strategies that you should use while taking the exam.

 THINK ABOUT IT: These tips are not necessarily tested concepts, but they provide background information to help make sense of concepts and give necessary information to help answer questions on the exam.

 CAUTION: Caution tips explain what to avoid when selecting your answer choices on the exam. Test writers are very good at creating distracting answer choices that seem like good options. We teach you what to watch for when it comes to distractors so you avoid these pitfalls.

Don't forget to look over the reference pages.

In the reference section, I have included a Good Words List you should review before taking the practice tests. This is a list of words, terms, and phrases that are typically in correct answer choices on this exam. There is also a Bad Words List, which contains words and phrases to avoid. Use the list to *think like a test maker, not a test taker* and to be strategic on the exam.

Along with the Good Words and Bad Words List, I have included extra info on comprehension and vocabulary instruction. There are also a list of main theorists and extra links in this section of the book. These resources will help you with any ESL or ESOL exam.

Six Principles of ESOL

I have included the six principles of ESOL here because if you keep these principles in mind, they will not only help you find correct answers on the exam, but they will also help you to be an effective ESOL/ESL teacher.

Principle 1: Know your learners.

Principle 2: Create conditions for language learning.

Principle 3: Design high-quality lessons for language development.

Principle 4: Adapt language delivery as needed.

Principle 5: Monitor and assess language development.

Principle 6: Engage and collaborate within a community of practice.

Acronyms Used in this Study Guide

When it comes to ESOL/ESL, there are many acronyms used to describe teachers, students, programs, approaches, and more. It is important to understand these acronyms, so below I have listed the most common ones used.

ELL – English Language Learner. This is the same as EL or English Learner. This is the term used for students whose first language is not English and who are learning English as a second language. **ELL** and **EL** are interchangeable terms. Therefore, whether your ESOL/ESL test uses ELL or EL, they both mean the same thing.

ESOL – English Speakers of Other Languages. This is similar to ELL and EL. However, ESOL is usually attached to the word program. For example, *Ms. Rodriguez is the ESOL teacher at my school* or *Our ESOL classes have several students from Central America and South America.*

ESL – English as a Second Language. This is like ESOL, and these acronyms are often used interchangeably. Some certification exams are called ESL certification. Just remember, ESOL and ESL are the same.

ELP – English Language Proficiency. This is a measure by which teachers determine the level of English proficiency a student has.

ELDS – English Language Development Standards. The WIDA English Language Development (ELD) Standards Framework provides a foundation for curriculum, instruction, and assessment for multilingual learners in kindergarten through grade 12. The ELD Standards Framework is centered on equity and fosters the assets, contributions, and potential of multilingual learners. You can see the 2020 standards on the WIDA website.

LEP – Limited English Proficiency. This acronym refers to students who are in the beginning stages of second language acquisition and who need support.

L1 – Language One. This is the first language. This is sometimes referred to as the home language or heritage language.

L2 – Language Two. This is the second language the student is learning in school. Because we are referring to schools in the United States, L2 is English.

This page intentionally left blank.

I - Standards-Based Instruction

Academic Standards

For all content areas and for all grade levels, there are a set of state academic standards teachers must follow. Educational standards are the learning goals for what students should know and be able to do at each grade level. These are not the curriculum. Instead, they are guides that the curriculum should follow.

Teachers must use the state standards to drive their instructional planning for all students, regardless of the students' first languages or countries of origin. The state standards are the benchmarks by which students are measured every year.

I recommend you look over the standards for your state, specifically the English language arts standards. In addition, the Common Core Standards outline what is required of students in the United States. You can access the Common Core English language art standards here: http://www.corestandards.org/ELA-Literacy/.

Caution

Beware of answer choices that lower the expectation or make things easier on the student. While teachers accommodate students and use scaffolding techniques to differentiate, practices like lowering the standards are usually not the correct answer choices.

WIDA – English Language Development Standards

Beyond the academic standards, there are national standards designed to help teachers assist students whose first language is not English.

World Class Instructional Design (WIDA) is a consortium of states dedicated to the design and implementation of high standards and equitable educational opportunities for English language learners (ELLs). Currently, 41 states belong to WIDA.

There are five main WIDA standards that provide educators with a connection between language development and academic content.

Standard 1 – Social and Instructional Language – English language learners communicate for social and instructional purposes within the school setting.

Standard 2 – Language of Language Arts – English language learners communicate information, ideas, and concepts necessary for academic success in the content area of language arts.

Standard 3 – Language of Mathematics – English language learners communicate information, ideas, and concepts necessary for academic success in the content area of mathematics.

Standard 4 – Language of Science – English language learners communicate information, ideas, and concepts necessary for academic success in the content area of science.

Standard 5 – Language of Social Studies – English language learners communicate information, ideas, and concepts necessary for academic success in the content area of social studies.

To learn more about WIDA, go to this website https://wida.wisc.edu/. There you will find many resources to help you be an effective ESOL/ESL instructor. In addition, the information on this website is beneficial for passing the ESOL/ESL certification exam.

Bloom's Taxonomy

When providing standards-based instruction and building objectives in the classroom, you should reference Bloom's Taxonomy.

Bloom's Taxonomy is a hierarchical model used to classify educational learning objectives into levels of complexity and specificity. The higher up the pyramid, the more complex the thinking skills. The skills are represented as verbs on the pyramid. When answering questions on the exam regarding critical thinking, reference Bloom's Taxonomy. The figure below is a modified version of Bloom's Taxonomy. We have modified it to include other skills (verbs) you may see on the exam.

Critical Thinking - This is multi-step, high-level thinking. Students are stretching in their thinking to analyze, evaluate, interpret, and synthesize information to reach a conclusion or make a judgment.

Creative Thinking - This requires students to create something by applying their skills. When students apply their skills, they are operating at a high cognitive level.

Reflective Thinking - Students look back on and reflect upon their learning process to promote abstract thinking and to encourage the application of learning strategies to new situations.

The skills (verbs) at the highest points of the pyramid are apply, evaluate, analyze, and create. When you are faced with a critical thinking problem on the test, visualize this pyramid, and look for answer choices that reflect the higher portions of the pyramid.

| Create |
| Analyze |
| Evaluate |
| Apply |
| Compare & Contrast |
| Categorize |
| Understand & Identify |
| Remember & Memorize |

(Modified Bloom's Taxonomy)

Autonomous Learning

Learner autonomy has been widely discussed in second language acquisition (SLA). Learner autonomy is the ability of the learners to take responsibility for their own learning. Students do this by using their self-reflection, critical thinking, and metacognition skills.

Metacognition is thinking about thinking. When students have metacognition, they understand the processes in their minds and can employ a variety of techniques to understand text.

Strategies for boosting **comprehension, critical thinking**, and **metacognition** are:

- *Predicting* - Asking students what they think will happen next.

- *Questioning* - Having students ask questions based on what they are reading.

- *Read aloud/think aloud* – The teacher or student reads and stops to think aloud about what the text means.

- *Summarizing* - Asking students to summarize.

Quick Tip

A valuable skill used in reading comprehension is metacognition. To develop metacognition skills, help students think about the processes they use in their brains as they read through text. We often take these processes for granted. However, when we are aware of what our brain is doing when we read, we can change the process or increase the process that helps us understand text.

Differentiation

The most effective teachers use instructional methods, resources, and materials appropriate for addressing specified instructional goals and promoting learning in students with diverse characteristics and needs. That means they differentiate instruction to accommodate learning preferences and student needs.

One of the most effective ways to differentiate for ELLs is to consider their stages of language acquisition. The following is a chart of the main stages of the way students acquire a new language.

STAGES OF SECOND LANGUAGE ACQUISITION	
Pre-production	The learner watches and listens to absorb the language. This stage is sometimes referred to as "the silent stage."
Early production	The learner starts to use some words but has not yet mastered forming sentences. Using pictures is helpful in this stage.
Speech emergence	The learner uses simple sentences that may or may not be correct. He or she begins to understand simple phrases in this stage.
Intermediate fluency	The learner has a much better grasp on the language as he/she begins to comprehend information taught in the second language and speaks in longer sentences.
Advanced fluency	The learner can speak and understand the new language with little to no support. This is when students demonstrate cognitive language proficiency to go beyond the basics and think/respond critically in the acquired language.

When considering the stages of language acquisition, the teacher can choose appropriate practices, activities, and assignments that match the students' levels of language.

Other ways to engage ELLs

- **Roleplay** – use real-world interaction to promote conversational language.

- **Dialect variation** – explain that even inside languages there are variations to consider when listening to someone speak.

- **Use visuals** – ELLs, especially those in the early production stage, benefit from visuals to support the text or conversation.

Students need variety in their learning experiences because students have different learning preferences, also known as multiple intelligences. For example, some students are read/write learners while others are visual learners. Some students prefer getting up and moving their bodies while others like to work in groups.

Homogeneous Groups

Everyone in the group has been identified as having the same learning need or are all at the same level. For example, a group of all level 3 readers. Homogenous groups should only be used temporarily to apply interventions. Homogeneous grouping should not be used as the primary grouping structure.

Heterogeneous Groups

Groups are formed so that there is a variety of learning levels and student interests. For example, grouping students by interest rather than reading scores will provide more diversity among the group members.

Students should only be placed in homogenous groups when a teacher is targeting a specific skill for a selected small group of students for remediation or enrichment. Heterogeneous grouping should be used for all other classroom activities.

Differentiated instruction. This is a framework for effective teaching that addresses learners' various needs (e.g., various abilities, strengths/weaknesses, and readiness). For example, the teacher makes sure the task suits the students' learning styles, is careful when grouping students, and uses authentic lessons and problem-based activities (Weselby, 2014).

- **Differentiated content -** This is when teachers have a variety of subjects based on students' interest or readiness. For example, based on leveled groups, students analyze poems at varying difficulty levels.

- **Differentiated process -** This is when a teacher modifies instruction to meet the various needs of the students in the class. This is often done using flexible groups. For example, after a short, whole-group lesson on metaphors, students split into small groups to analyze concepts.

Student-Centered Learning

The term student-centered learning refers to a wide variety of educational programs, learning experiences, instructional approaches, and academic-support strategies that are intended to address the distinct learning needs, interests, aspirations, or cultural backgrounds of individual students and groups of students. To accomplish this goal, educators use a variety of educational methods, such as modifying assignments and instructional strategies in the classroom and redesigning the ways in which students are grouped and taught in school (The Glossary of Education Reform, 2019).

In a student-centered environment, teachers pay attention to learning preferences, readiness levels, and developmentally appropriate practices. Below are considerations when designing a student-centered or learner-centered classroom environment. This is also called using different modalities.

- **Visual learners –** These students thrive when the learning is accompanied by images and graphics to organize information.

- **Auditory learners –** These students grasp concepts best through listening and speaking situations (think lectures and podcasts).

- **Kinesthetic leaners –** These students prefer hands-on learning experiences and moving their bodies.

- **Read and write learners –** These students prefer reading and writing activities to make sense of abstract concepts.

Think Like a Test Maker

Increase wait time for ELLs. This involves giving the students time to think and formulate an answer, which is especially important when asking high-level questions. This is especially helpful for ELLs as they may need additional time to think in L2.

Measurable Objectives

Learning objectives are the behavior or skills students are expected to acquire in a lesson. These objectives should be measurable, meaning teachers should be able to determine if the objective is met either by a formative or summative assessment. We will discuss assessment in the following sections. Measurable objectives allow teachers to determine if students understand the lesson and are meeting the standards.

Backwards Design

When planning lessons, backwards design is very effective. The key to backwards design is to start with the state standards and work backwards.

Alignment is critical. Start with the standards, plan the assessments, monitor the students' progress at key intervals, and adjust short-term objectives accordingly.

Steps to Backwards Design

1. Identify the state adopted standards for the concepts you are teaching. Be sure you are following the scope and sequence outlined by the state standards. The goal is student mastery of the standard(s).

2. Choose what assessments you will use to determine if the students mastered the standard(s).

3. Plan the lesson and activities.

4. Monitor progress as students move through the unit, lesson, or activity.

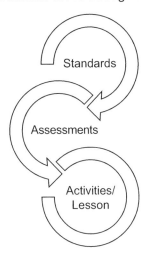

- Start with the state adopted standards. That is the end goal–to have the students master the standard(s).

- Determine how you will know the students mastered the standard and what assessments you will use to measure success.

- Decide what lessons and activities you will have students engage in to work toward standards mastery.

Know the difference between long-term goals, which typically happen over the course of a semester of year, and short-term goals, which typically happen within a month or grading period, and how to apply goals to the instructional planning process.

Flexibility

Another important element of effective lesson plans is fluidity. Lessons do not always go according to plan. For example, it may take longer than expected for ELLs to understand a concept or complete an activity. Therefore, lesson plans should be flexible, and teachers should modify the lessons according to students' needs.

The Four Domains of Language

It is important that you understand the four domains of language for any ESL or ESOL exam. They are:

1. Listening

2. Speaking

3. Reading

4. Writing

Quick Tip

In the pullout ESL program, English language learners are pulled out of regular, mainstream classrooms for special instruction in English as a second language. In contrast, the push-in ESL program brings the ESL teacher into the regular mainstream classroom to provide ESL instruction to a group of students.

Typically, students acquire these skills in the order indicated above. First students learn to listen in the second language. Then they learn to speak in the second language. Then they read in the second language. The last skill is writing in the second language.

1. **Listening vocabulary** – First students acquire listening vocabulary. Listening vocabulary refers to the words we need to know to understand what we hear. This is part of students' receptive vocabulary.

2. **Speaking vocabulary** – Next, students acquire speaking vocabulary. Speaking vocabulary consists of the words we use when we speak. This is part of students' expressive vocabulary.

3. **Reading vocabulary** – Next, students acquire reading vocabulary. Reading vocabulary refers to the words we need to know to understand what we read. This is part of students' receptive vocabulary.

Think Like a Test Maker

L1 stands for the first language, and L2 stands for the second language. Remember, proficiency in L1 directly impacts proficiency in L2, meaning a student will do well in the second language if she has strong skills in her first language. Keep that in mind when answering questions for this exam.

4. **Writing vocabulary** – The last skill acquired is writing vocabulary. Writing vocabulary consists of the words we use in writing. This is part of students' expressive vocabulary.

Listening comprehension – This skill relates to listening vocabulary. When students have listening comprehension, they can understand a story that is being read aloud. Students will often develop their listening comprehension before their reading comprehension.

Receptive Skills vs. Expressive Skills		
Receptive	Reading, Listening	Listening to a book on tape, reading an article
Expressive	Speaking, Writing	Engaging in role play, writing a poem

Quick Tip

Basic Interpersonal Communication Skills (BICS) refer to linguistic skills needed in everyday social face-to-face interactions.

Cognitive Academic Language Proficiency (CALP) focuses on academic language or language used in the classroom.

I – Standards-Based Instruction Practice Questions

1. Which of the following is the correct progression of vocabulary acquisition in ELs?

   A. Listening vocabulary, speaking vocabulary, reading vocabulary, writing vocabulary

   B. Speaking vocabulary, listening vocabulary, reading vocabulary, writing vocabulary

   C. Listening vocabulary, reading vocabulary, speaking vocabulary, writing vocabulary

   D. Speaking vocabulary, reading vocabulary, listening vocabulary, writing vocabulary

2. An ELL uses some words in L2 and relies on pictures to help recognize L2 vocabulary. What stage of second language acquisition is this student in?

   A. Pre-production

   B. Early production

   C. Speech emergent

   D. Intermediate fluency

   E. Advanced fluency

3. Which of the following is true about the relationship between oral development and literacy development during second language acquisition (SLA)?

   A. Oral language and literacy development are not related.

   B. Literacy development precedes oral language development.

   C. Oral language development precedes literacy development.

   D. Oral language development depends on literacy development.

4. Which of the following has a direct impact on a student's second language literacy development?

   A. Literacy development in L1

   B. Proficiency level in L2

   C. Comprehension

   D. Fluency

5. A teacher has several ELLs in class, and all have varying levels of reading proficiency. What can the teacher do to ensure all students are achieving?

   A. Group students based on ability in L2 and continue instruction throughout the year based on those groups.

   B. Have the advanced ELLs tutor the struggling ELLs during cooperative learning sessions.

   C. Communicate to parents that at-home practice in L2 is essential in helping students achieve.

   D. Differentiate instruction based on data and continuously challenge students with higher-order thinking activities.

6. Ms. Smith wants her students to incorporate at-home reading practice in L2 as part of their literacy plan. What would be the most effective approach moving forward?

    A. Provide parents with reading comprehension questions to ask students after reading.

    B. Provide parents with short reading activities to do with students for at-home practice.

    C. Have students keep a reading log to track their reading every night.

    D. Reward students with extra time in the library for meeting their at-home reading goals.

7. Which of the following would be most effective when increasing literacy skills in L2?

    A. Have students read in L2 until they master literacy in L2.

    B. Have students master all skills in L1 before moving on to literacy skills in L2.

    C. Activate students' prior knowledge and use relevant literature.

    D. Allow students to decide what they learn.

8. Which of the following has the most impact on a student's second language acquisition?

    A. Socioeconomic status

    B. Standardized test scores

    C. Classroom placement

    D. Frequency of L2 used at home

9. Which of the following should be the focus of literacy development?

    A. Memorizing vocabulary words in L2

    B. Thinking critically in L1 and L2

    C. Using a dictionary to help with translation

    D. Learning cooperatively in L2

10. What can a teacher do to help an ELL who has just entered the classroom and is in the pre-production stage of language acquisition?

    A. Require the student to start speaking English as soon as possible.

    B. Consistently change the student's peer group so she gets to know everyone.

    C. Provide the student with an English to Spanish dictionary for testing purposes.

    D. Honor the silent period and provide safe times to speak academic English.

Number	Answer	Explanation
1.	A	**Listening vocabulary** – First, students acquire listening vocabulary. Listening vocabulary refers to the words we need to know to understand what we hear. This is part of students' receptive vocabulary. **Speaking vocabulary** – Next, students acquire speaking vocabulary. Speaking vocabulary consists of the words we use when we speak. This is part of students' expressive vocabulary. **Reading vocabulary** – Next, students acquire reading vocabulary. Reading vocabulary refers to the words we need to know to understand what we read. This is part of students' receptive vocabulary. **Writing vocabulary** – The last skill acquired is writing vocabulary. Writing vocabulary consists of the words we use in writing. This is part of students' expressive vocabulary.
2.	B	A. **Pre-production** – The learner watches and listens to absorb the language. Referred to as "the silent stage." B. **Early production** – The learner starts to use some words but has not yet mastered forming sentences. Using pictures (just as in first language acquisition) is helpful in this stage. C. **Speech emergence** – The learner uses simple sentences that may or may not be correct. He or she begins to understand simple phrases in this stage. D. **Intermediate fluency** – The learner has a much better grasp on the language as he or she begins to comprehend information taught in the second language and speaks in longer sentences. E. **Advanced fluency** – The learner can speak and understand the new language with little to no support. This is when students demonstrate cognitive language proficiency to go beyond the basics and think and respond critically in the acquired language.
3.	C	This question is testing your ability to know that students learn to speak a language before they read and write in that language. This is true for first and second languages. Most often, humans learn to listen and speak, then read and write.
4.	A	Students' literacy proficiency in their first language directly impacts their proficiency in their second language. This is important to keep in mind throughout the exam. Many questions will assess this concept. Students who struggle with literacy in their first language will most likely face challenges in L2. Conversely, those who excel in L1 will most likely excel in L2.

Standards-Based Instruction

Number	Answer	Explanation
5.	D	Answer D has all the good words in it. Differentiating instruction based on data is most often the correct answer. Answer A is incorrect because grouping students based on ability should only be done temporarily for interventions, not for the entire year. Answer B is incorrect because you should not rely on other students to tutor struggling students. Finally, answer C is incorrect because relying on parents to close the achievement gap is inappropriate. This should be done at school.
6.	B	This question is testing your knowledge of students' home language use (L1). To increase L2 acquisition, it is beneficial to read at home in L2. The most effective approach is to involve the parents in a way that is not overwhelming. A list of comprehension questions is not the most effective approach here. However, short reading activities that are manageable for the parent is the best approach.
7.	C	Whenever thinking about literacy development, activating prior knowledge and using text that is relevant to students' lives is always the correct answer. You may be tempted to choose answer B; however, the student does not have to master all the skills in L1 to read in L2. Rather, the teacher should support both L1 and L2 while the student is learning the second language.
8.	D	The more students interact with L2 the more quickly they will learn L2. The other answer choices do not impact L2 development.
9.	B	Critical thinking is the reason we teach literacy. In addition, helping students to think critically is the goal of school. Therefore, if you see critical thinking in an answer choice, slow down and take a closer look because it is most likely the correct answer.
10.	D	Teachers must honor this period and provide a safe place for students to try L2. All the other answer choices are negative in nature, so avoid those. Also, switching a new student's group can cause anxiety. Try to keep things simple and consistent for students who are in the pre-production stage of language acquisition.

Phonetics

Understanding phonetics will help ESL instructors, especially those who are teaching speaking skills. Consider the following:

- How can we break sounds into smaller components? (morphology)

- Can two sounds sound the same to speakers of one language and be different to speakers of another language?

- How can stress be a significant factor in language acquisition?

- Why might an L2 learner say, *He talk-ed* rather than *He talkt* for "He talked"?

- How does stress change the meanings of the marked words: He is in a *high*chair. He is in a high *chair*.

These are all circumstances of the English language that can present challenges to ELLs and ESOL teachers.

Universal Language Principles

There are certain principles, rules, and instances in language that span most languages all over the world. For example, adjectives, verbs, and nouns may have different names in different languages, but their functions are the same. Language is rule governed, systematic, and arbitrary.

- **Language is rule-governed** – Most languages are governed by grammar where there are patterns and rules the language follows.

- **Language is systematic** – This is the letter to sound relationship in words. This is known as phonics (spelling) in English.

- **Language is arbitrary** – The sounds in language have nothing to do with meaning. They are essentially random sounds cultures use to make words.

International Phonetic Alphabet (IPA)

The international phonetic alphabet (IPA) is a system of phonetic notation based on Latin. It was developed by the International Phonetic Association in the late 1800s as a standardized representation of speech sounds in written form. The IPA is used by lexicographers (people who write dictionaries), foreign language students and teachers, linguists, speech–language pathologists, singers, actors, constructed language creators, and translators (Wall, 1989).

The IPA is designed to represent qualities of speech that are part of sounds in oral language: phones, phonemes, intonation, and the separation of words and syllables. The IPA represents these sounds with different symbols.

The following tables represent the symbols and sounds of the IPA. While it is not necessary to memorize these sounds for the exam, it does help to understand these different representations.

Consonant Sounds										
p	pat	[pæt]		θ	thick	[θɪk]		dʒ	judge	[dʒədʒ]
b	bat	[bæt]		ð	the	[ðə]		m	mat	[mæt]
t	pat	[pæt]		s	sat	[sæt]		n	gnat	[næt]
d	pad	[pæd]		z	zip	[zɪp]		ŋ	sing	[sɪŋ]
k	cat	[kæt]		ʃ	wash	[waʃ]		l	last	[læst]
g	get	[gɛt]		ʒ	garage	[gəraʒ]		r	rat	[ræt]
f	fat	[fæt]		h	hat	[hæt]		w	what	[wət]
v	vat	[væt]		tʃ	match	[mætʃ]		j	yet	[jɛt]

Vowel Sounds										
i	sheep		i	ship		ʊ	good		ü	shoot
e	bed		ə	teacher		ɜ	bird		ɔ	door
æ	cat		ʌ	up		a	far		ɒ	on

Schwa

Probably one of the most confusing parts of English is the use of the schwa (ə) sound. It is sometimes referred to as the reduced vowel sound in a word. Even though most people do not know about shwa, it is the most widely used vowel sound in spoken English. Schwa is a quick, relaxed, and neutral way of pronouncing vowels. Schwa allows speakers to pronounce unstressed syllables, so the main beats of spoken words are easier to place on the stressed syllables. Below are a few examples of words that use the Schwa (underlined portion in the words).

Vowel	Word 1	Explanation
A	again	Notice that the second *a* in this word is relaxed. We do not usually pronounce the second *a* as a long *a*. We just let the sound lazily come out.
E	problem	The *e* sound is not fully pronounced in this word. It sort of just falls out of the mouth. We do not fully pronounce the *e* sound.
i	duplicate	Notice the lazy *i* sound is pronounced very quickly in two parts of the word (for the *i* and the *a*). We do not pronounce *i* or long *a* sound (unless *duplicate* is used as a verb). Instead, both are quick short *i* vowel sounds, as in: The book was a *duplicate* copy.

Vowel	Word 1	Explanation
O	parlor	The **o** sound in this word has an **er** sound. We usually do not pronounce the **o** in the ending.
U	suppose	The **u** sound is short and quick when pronouncing this word.
Y	analysis	We do not pronounce the **y** fully in this word. It has more of a lazy short **i** sound.

Dialect vs. Accent

Dialect and accent are two different aspects of language.

An *accent* is also specific to a region. In English, there might be an American, British, or Australian accent. An accent is an inflection that occurs with word pronunciation.

A *dialect* is using entirely different words or ways of communicating altogether. Dialect goes beyond mere pronunciation.

Caution

It is not necessary for you to memorize all the sounds and their symbols for most ESOL/ESL teacher certification exams. Rather, you should understand that the IPA exists and is used when teaching second language learners.

Dialects

A dialect is a particular form of a language specific to a region or social group. It is important to consider dialect when teaching ESOL. Remember, ESOL students are not a monolith, and English speakers are not a monolith. English is spoken differently in different parts of the country. Therefore, dialect is an important consideration when teaching ELLs.

Here are examples of dialects in America that ELLs might need clarification on:

- Soda vs. Pop
- Howdy vs. Hello

Stress and Intonation Patterns

There are two very basic rules when it comes to word stress patterns in English:

- A word only has *one* stress.
- We only stress vowels in words.

Sometimes you'll see stress patterns represented as dots. The dots represent the syllables in words. The big dots are the stressed syllable.

There are 3 types of stress in words.

1. Primary stress: the loudest syllable in the word.
2. Secondary stress: syllables which aren't completely unstressed but aren't as loud as the primary stress.
3. Unstressed syllables: syllables that have no stress at all.

General Stress Rules (ETS – TOEFL, 2015)

Examples of Stress Patterns	
Geographic	●● **●** ●
Climate	**●** ●
Elevation	●● **●** ●

Stress the first syllable of:

- Most two-syllable nouns (examples: CLImate, KNOWledge)
- Most two-syllable adjectives (examples: FLIPpant, SPAcious)

Stress the last syllable of:

- Most two-syllable verbs (examples: reQUIRE, deCIDE)

Stress the second-to-last syllable of:

- Words that end in -ic (examples: ecSTATic, geoGRAPHic)
- Words ending in -sion and -tion (examples: exTENsion, retriBUtion)

Stress the third-from-last syllable of:

- Words that end in -cy, -ty, -phy and -gy (examples: deMOCracy, unCERtainty, geOGraphy, radiOLogy)
- Words that end in -al (examples: exCEPtional, CRItical)

Think Like a Test Maker

Epenthesis means the addition of one or more sounds to a word, especially to the interior of a word. A student who pronounces the word "sport" as [ɛ sport] *eh sport* adds one sound to the initial syllable of the word. The following is an example.

My favorite eh sport is soccer.

Voice vs. Voiceless Sounds

In English, some sounds require the use of our voice while others do not. To test this, you can put your fingers gently on your voice box while saying the following sounds. For voiced sounds, you will feel a vibration. For voiceless sounds, you will not feel a vibration.

Voiced Consonants

b, d, g, z, m, n, ng, i, r, w, y, -si- (explosion), *j* (joke). The consontants *th* are usually voiced when they are at the beginning of the word as in *that*.

Voiceless consonants

p, t, s, k, h, th, sh, ch (cheese). The *d* at the end of words as in *bed*.

It is important to remember that voiced vs, voiceless consonants are influenced by where they are in the word and the vowels around them. For example, the *th* in the word *that* is voiced. However, the *th* in the word *bath* is not.

Sentence Stress Patterns

Of coursse, not all sentences or words follow every rule. However, below are the general rules for stressing parts of sentences.

Stress content words such as nouns, verbs, adjectives, and adverbs.

Stress negative words as in *not* **or** *never*. These words are stressed because they affect the meaning of the sentence. Modals or axillary verbs can also change the meaning of a sentence. Therefore, they are also stressed. As a general rule, stress the following:

- nouns (people, places, things)
- verbs (actions, states)
- adjectives (words that modify nouns)
- adverbs (words that modify verbs, adjectives, other adverbs, or entire sentences)
- negative words (*not, never, neither*, etc.)
- modals (*should, could, might, must*)
- *yes, no,* and auxiliary verbs in short answers (e.g., **Yes**, *she* **does**.)
- quantifiers (*some, many, no, all, one, two, three*, etc.)
- question words that start with the *wh-* (*what, where, when, why, how*). However, *what* sometimes breaks this rule when speaking quickly as in *What's up?*

Quick Tip

Not all verbs are the same. You should understand the difference between auxiliary verbs and modal verbs.

Auxiliary verbs are considered helping verbs and are used to add tense, mood, and voice. For example, in the sentence below, the helping verb ***have*** adds mood. The words *be, have* and *do* are considered auxiliary verbs.

Ex: We ***have*** been to Europe.

Modal verbs express possibility or necessity. The words *can, could, may, might, must, ought to, shall, should, will, would*, and *need* are modal verbs.

Ex: We ***must*** go to the hospital now to see Dad.

Phonological Awareness, Phonemic Awareness & Phonics

Phonological awareness is an overarching skill that includes identifying and manipulating units of oral language, including parts of words, syllables, onsets, and rimes.

ELLs who have phonological awareness can:

- identify and make oral rhymes.
- clap the number of syllables in a word.
- recognize words with the same initial sounds like <u>m</u>onkey and <u>m</u>other.
- recognize the sound of spoken language.
- blend sounds together (*bl, tr, sk*).
- divide and manipulate words.

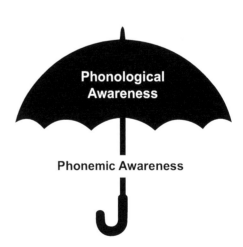

Phonemic awareness is understanding the individual sounds (or phonemes) in words. For example, students who have phonemic awareness can separate the sounds in the word *cat* into three distinct phonemes: /k/, /æ/, and /t/.

Phonics is understanding the relationship between sounds and the spelling patterns (graphemes) representing those sounds. For example, when a student sees the letter *c* is followed by an *e, i,* or *y,* the student knows the *c* makes an /s/ sound, as in the words *cycle, circle,* and *receive*.

The difference between phonemic awareness and phonics skills.

Phonemic awareness includes the skills that encompass using sounds in words. When you think phonemic awareness, think of sounds only. For example, if students are recognizing individual sounds in words or blending sounds in words without having to see the word, it is phonemic awareness.

Phonics is understanding letter/sound correspondence. Students must see the letters or words to engage in phonics. For example, in the word **receive**, students know the *c* makes an /s/ sound because the *c* is followed by an *e, i,* or *y*. That is a basic example of letter/sound correspondence.

Quick Tip

Think of phonological awareness as the umbrella encompassing many skills students need for literacy: syllabication, onsets, rimes, spelling, etc. Phonemic awareness is a more nuanced skill that requires students to understand individual sounds in words.

Phonemic Awareness	Phonics
Focus on phonemes/sounds	Focus on graphemes/letters and their corresponding sounds
Spoken language	Written language/print
Mostly auditory	Both visual and auditory
Manipulating sounds in words	Reading and writing letters according to sounds, spelling, patterns, and phonological structure

(Heggerty, 2003)

Morphology

Morphology is the study of word parts and their meanings. Morphemes are the smallest units of meaning in a word. For example, in the word *unbelievable*, there are three morphemes—*un* (not), *believe* (trust), *able* (capable). The following list provides categories and examples of using morphology to develop decoding skills.

- **Compound words.** Two words put together.

    Example: *mailman, sidewalk*

Think about it!

When students use morphemes to decode words, they are usually using prefixes, suffixes, and roots. They will also break apart compound words. This is also referred to as a structural analysis because students are breaking down the morphemic structure of the word to figure out its meaning.

- **Root words.** The root of a word is the basic part of the word. It stands alone in meaning and in English language often comes from Latin languages.

    Example: In the word *unbelievable*, the root word is *believe*. In the word *complex*, the root word is *plex*.

- **Prefixes.** Additions to root words that help to form a new word with another meaning from that of the root word. Prefixes are at the beginning of a word.

    Example: Prefixes that indicate not: *un-* (unknown), *dis-* (disregard), im-(impossible), *in-* (inaccurate), *mis-*(misunderstand), and *ir-* (irrational).

- **Suffixes.** Additions to root words that form a new word with another meaning from that of the root word. Suffixes are at the end of a word. They change the part of speech (past tense, present tense) or verb tense of a word. They also indicate whether the word is plural or singular.

    Example: *-ed, -ing,* and plural *-s* are all suffixes

Students can break words down to even smaller pieces by focusing on letter sound relationships. For example, words can be broken down by:

- inflected forms (*-s, -es, -ed, -ing, -ly*)
- contractions
- possessives
- compound words
- syllables
- base words

- root words
- prefixes
- suffixes beginning consonants
- end consonants
- medial consonants
- consonant blends (*bl, gr, sp*)

- consonant digraphs (*sh, th, ch*)
- short vowels
- long vowels
- vowel pairs (*oo, ew, oi, oy*)

Free Morphemes – These morphemes can stand alone because they mean something in and of themselves. For example, in the word ***closely***, the morpheme ***close*** is a free morpheme. It can stand alone.

Quick Tip

Remember, the spelling of a suffix can vary depending on its root word. For example, the suffixes *able* and *ible* both mean capable.

- Use the *–able* ending if the root word is not changed like in *comfort – comfortable*.
- Use the *–able* ending if there is a related word that ends in *–ation*, as in *consideration – considerable*.
- Use the *–ible* ending when you can't hear a whole root word like in *invisible*.

Bound Morphemes – These morphemes only have meaning when they are connected to another morpheme. In the word ***closely,*** the morpheme ***ly*** cannot stand on its own and only has meaning when it is attached to another morpheme.

According to Pearson (2010), readers use multilettered groups in word structure to:

- Automatically recognize and pronounce large, intact letter groups in long words.
- Use word parts to indicate meaning—for example, the prefix *un-* in unhappy, the suffix *-ly* in friendly, and the root word *sign* in *signal* and *signature*.

- Use syllables as units of pronunciation, such as the syllables *dis*, *trib*, and *ute* in distribute.
- Using strategies for analyzing long words to find useful multilettered groups is more efficient than other word identification strategies.

To sum this up, readers can use morphology to chunk words, separate words, and organize words so readers can develop fluency and comprehension.

Quick Tip

A chunk is a group of letters that represents meaning and sound (the *re* in *regroup* or the *un* and *able* in *unbelievable*).

Explicit Phonics Instruction

The following table includes examples of how teachers and students can use letter sound correspondence, spelling conventions, and graphemes to teach literacy. This information was adapted from the Common Core State Standards for English Language Arts and Literacy - Appendix A.

Grapheme Type	Definition	Examples
Single letters	A single consonant letter can be represented by a phoneme.	b, d, f, g, h, j, k, l, m, n, p, r, s, t, v, w, y, z
Doublets	A doublet uses two of the same letter to spell a consonant phoneme.	ff, ll, ss, zz
Digraphs	Digraphs are two-letter (di-) combinations that create one phoneme.	th, sh, ch, wh, ph, ng (sing) gh (cough) ck
Trigraphs	Trigraphs are three-letter (tri-) combinations that create one phoneme.	-tch -dge
Diphthong	Diphthongs are sounds formed by the combination of two vowels in a single syllable, in which the sound begins as one vowel and moves toward another. They can appear in the initial, middle, or final position in a word.	aisle coin loud
Consonant blends	Consonant blends include two or three graphemes, and the consonant sounds are separate and identifiable.	s-c-r (scrape) c-l (clean) l-k (milk)
Silent letter combinations	Silent letter combinations use two letters: one represents the phoneme and the other is silent.	kn (knock) wr (wrestle) gn (gnarl)

Think Like a Test Maker

Grapheme Type	Definition	Examples
Combination qu	These two letters always go together and make a /kw/ sound.	**qu**ickly
Single letters	A single vowel letter that stands for a vowel sound.	(short vowels) cat, hit, gem, pot, sub (long vowels) me, no, mute
Vowel teams	Vowel teams are combinations of two, three, or four letters that stand for a vowel sound.	(short vowels) head, hook (long vowels) boat, rain, weigh (diphthongs) soil, bout

Foundation of Linguistics

Consonant-Vowel Patterns

Other strategies for helping students decode words involve following common consonant-vowel patterns (CVC, CVCC, CVCe, CVVC patterns).

Pattern	Description	Example
CVC	consonant-vowel-consonant	bat, cat, tap
CVCe	consonant-vowel-consonant-silent e	make, take, bake
CCVC	consonant-consonant-vowel-consonant	trap, chop, grit
CVCC	consonant-vowel-consonant-consonant	tack, hunt, fast

Think Like a Test Maker

Be sure you understand inflectional morphemes. Foundational skills include understanding inflectional endings (-s, -es, -ed, -ing). This is part of morphology.

- -s or -es makes the word plural
- -ed makes the word past tense
- -ing implies the action is happening right now

High-frequency or sight words are words that show up in text very frequently. Students should memorize these words because it helps them save their cognitive endurance for more difficult reading tasks.

- want
- what
- why
- walk
- talk
- not
- saw
- say

- said
- see
- there
- those
- been
- because
- ever
- every

- by
- are
- would
- should
- water
- called
- over
- only

Teachers can provide students with opportunities to build and extend their phonics skills in a variety of ways. The most important way is to expose students to a variety of literary and informational text. The more print students are exposed to, the more words they learn and the more comfortable they become with their phonics skills.

Think Like a Test Maker

One of the only times memorization is a good practice is when increasing students' automaticity. This is done through memorizing high-frequency words.

Cueing Systems

As students begin to read, they use different methods to figure out words. Cueing systems allow students to use their background knowledge (schema) and apply that to understanding words. There are several types of cues students use when they read.

Semantic Cues

Semantic cues refer to the meaning in language that assists in comprehending texts, including words, speech, signs, symbols, and other meaning-bearing forms. Semantic cues involve the learners' prior knowledge of language. Gradually, students independently relate new information to what is known and personally meaningful.

Semantic cues are especially helpful for homographs—words that are spelled the same but have different meaning.

- For example: Thinking about leaving her friends made Jane blue.

The word *blue* in context is not the color but rather the feeling of sadness. Semantic cues help the student understand this.

Syntactic Cues

Syntactic cues involve the structure of the word as in the rules and patterns of language (grammar) and punctuation. As students read, they use structural cues.

- Example: Joey *sat* in class yesterday.

In this case, the student is sure to say *sat* not *sit* because of the word yesterday indicates there needs to be a past tense verb—*sat*.

Think Like a Test Maker

Remember, readers' oral vocabulary knowledge helps them derive meaning as they decode words. Vocabulary knowledge supports the semantic cueing system.

Graphophonic Cues

Graphophonic cues involve the letter-sound or sound-symbol relationships of language. Readers identifying unknown words by relating speech sounds to letters or letter patterns are using graphophonic cues. This process is often called decoding.

Pragmatic Cues (Important for L2 acquisition)

These cues are very important because they have to do with the social use of language. For example, "*Excuse me*" in contemporary American English has taken on a function of getting someone who is blocking the way to move.

- **Greetings:** *How are you? How's it going?*

- **Closings:** *See you later. Have a great day.*

Social Linguistics

Social linguistics is the study of language in relation to social factors, including differences of regional, class, and occupational dialect, gender differences, and bilingualism.

- **Rhetorical patterns** – ways of organizing information. Rhetoric refers to the way people use language to process information. Examples of rhetorical patterns are:

Cause and effect	Compare and contrast
Argument and persuasion	Definition
Classification	Description
Chronological/sequential	

- **Active voice** – Active voice is most appropriate in writing. Active voice is when the subject of a sentence performs the verb's action. Sentences in the active voice have a strong, direct, and clear tone. For example:

  - The superintendent gave the man permission to leave early.

  - The man attacked the woman.

  - The legislators did not pass the bill.

- **Passive voice** – Writers should avoid passive voice because sentences in the passive voice have a weak and indirect tone. In passive voice, the verb is acting upon the subject and can cause confusion. For example:

  - The man was given permission to leave early.

  - The woman was attacked.

  - The bill was not passed.

- **Transfer from L1 to L2** – In many cases, ELLs will transfer their knowledge in L1 to L2. This can be both positive and negative.

  - Positive transfer refers to the processes whereby L1 knowledge facilitates the acquisition of an L2.

  - Negative transfer refers to the processes whereby L1 knowledge interferes with and, thus, negatively impacts L2 acquisition.

Quick Tip

ELLs will often make mistakes in their prepositions when speaking English. For example, an ELL might say, "When we arrive to the party..." instead of "When we arrive at the party..." Another example is, "Claire goes out in night for work," instead of "Claire goes out at night for work."

Determining and Differentiating English Language Proficiency (ELP)

When working with ELLs, highly effective teachers apply knowledge of individual differences such as developmental characteristics, cultural and language background, academic strengths, and learning styles. The best teachers select focused, targeted, and systematic second language acquisition instruction to ELLs who are at the beginning or intermediate level of English-language proficiency in reading, and/or writing in accordance with the English Language Development Standards (ELDS).

ELP stands for English language proficiency, and it is an assessment that measures students' listening, reading, writing, and speaking skills.

Teachers can provide students with opportunities to build and extend their phonics skills in a variety of ways. The most important way is to expose students to a variety of literary and informational text. The more print students are exposed to, the more words they learn and the more comfortable they become with their phonics skills.

Teachers can also use:

- **Decodable texts** – texts that are intentionally sequenced to gradually incorporate words that are consistent with the letter–sound relationships that have been taught to the new reader or ELL.

- **Authentic and shared reading tasks** – an interactive reading experience where the teacher guides ELLs as they read text. The teacher explicitly models proficient reading skills, including reading with fluency and expression.

- **Oral reading** – when students read aloud in class, to a partner, in cooperative groups, or with a teacher.

- **Whisper reading** – instead of reading out loud or silently, ELLs read in a whisper voice. This allows ELLs to make mistakes without feeling embarrassed. It also helps students with decoding and fluency.

- **Word walls** - a literacy tool composed of an organized collection of words which are displayed in large visible letters on a wall, bulletin board, or other display surface in a classroom. These will be discussed further in the vocabulary section of the study guide.

- **Interactive writing** – when students and teacher share the process of writing. The teacher begins by writing a word or a piece of a word, and the student continues.

Think Like a Test Maker

In every blueprint and test specification for most ESL or ESOL certification exams, there is a section that addresses differentiated instruction for students who struggle, students who are English learners, students with disabilities, and students who are highly proficient. It is important that for every section of this test you are keeping all students in mind when it comes to teaching reading.

- For ELLs, supporting them in their first language and providing them with supports like graphic representation is effective in differentiating instruction.

- For ELLs with disabilities, it is imperative that you read their individual education plan (IEP) and be sure to accommodate these students based on what is in the plan.

- For ELLs who are above grade level or highly proficient, it is important that you challenge these students and continuously improve their skills.

Words like *differentiation, scaffolding, enrichment*, and *supports* are good words when it comes to these objectives.

Alphabetic principle

The alphabetic principle is the idea that letters and letter patterns represent the sounds of spoken language. Learning that there are predictable relationships among sounds and letters allows ELLs to apply these relationships to both familiar and unfamiliar words and to begin to read with fluency.

To promote the alphabetic principle, teachers should:

- Teach letter-sound relationships explicitly and in isolation.

- Provide opportunities for ELLs to practice letter-sound relationships in daily lessons.

- Provide practice opportunities that include new sound-letter relationships, as well as cumulatively reviewing previously taught relationships.

- Use writing or print to represent what students say during class, so students understand speech can be represented in print.

Teaching students to spell phonetically

Some words are spelled exactly how they sound. For example, *cat* is spelled exactly how it sounds. However, the word *phone* is not spelled exactly how it sounds.

When students are learning the alphabetic principle, they are using phonetic spelling—spelling words exactly how they sound. Phonetic spelling is essential in learning how to read and write, and teachers should encourage students to spell phonetically. Teachers can help students enhance their phonetic spelling by using the following practices.

- Introduce sound-letter relationships at a reasonable pace, in a range from two to four letter-sound relationships a week.

Think Like a Test Maker

Often, ELLs will overgeneralize when learning L2 and apply English rules to all words. We know that English sometimes does not follow its own rules. For example, irregular verbs do not follow the normal past tense rules, as in *to go* is not *goed* but *went*. The past tense of sleep is not *sleeped* but *slept*. When an ELL says *sleeped* instead of *slept*, they are overgeneralizing.

- Teach high-utility letter-sound relationships early. For example, the letters *m, a, t, s, p,* and *h* are high utility, but the letters *x* as in *box*, *gh*, as in *neighbor* are low utility.

- Provide student with the opportunities to read phonetically spelled words.

Understand the connection between spoken and written language.

Oral language consists of six major areas: phonology, vocabulary, morphology, grammar, pragmatics, and discourse.

1. **Phonology** encompasses the organization of sounds in language.

2. **Vocabulary** (semantics) encompasses both expressive (speaking) and receptive (listening) vocabulary.

3. **Morphology** is the study of the smallest units of meaning in words. An example of morphology is breaking up compound words and analyzing their meaning.

4. **Grammar** (syntax) is the structure of language and words.

5. **Pragmatics** focuses on the social cues or norms in language. This is often referred to as situations in language.

6. **Discourse** focuses on speaking and listening skills in language. Discourse means dialogue.

ELLs at the beginning (emergent) stage are learning to read and understand words by decoding the reading process as they engage with the text. Emergent literacy involves the skills, knowledge, and attitudes that are developmental precursors to conventional forms of reading and writing (Whitehurst & Lonigan, 1998).

The role of phonological processing in reading development of individual students and English learners.

Phonological processing is when students use phonemes to process spoken and written language (Wagner & Torgesen, 1987). Phonological processing includes *phonological awareness, phonological working memory*, and *phonological retrieval*.

It is very important that teachers develop the following skills in all students, including those students who struggle and those who are ELLs. Teachers can do this by differentiating instruction and helping ELLs develop phonemic awareness in their first language so they can develop these skills in their second language.

Phonological Awareness

Phonological awareness is the awareness of the sound structure of a language and the ability to consciously analyze and manipulate this structure via a range of tasks, such as speech sound segmentation and blending at the word, onset-rime, syllable, and phonemic levels.

Phonological Working Memory

Phonological working memory involves storing phoneme information in temporary, short-term memory (Wagner & Torgesen, 1987). This phonemic information is then readily available for manipulation during phonological awareness tasks. For example, when students use substitution, they are also using their phonological working memory because they are accessing stored phoneme information to substitute sounds in words.

Phonological Retrieval

Phonological retrieval is the ability to recall the phonemes associated with specific graphemes, which can be assessed by rapid naming tasks (e.g., rapid naming of letters and numbers). This ability to recall the speech sounds in one's language is also integral to phonological awareness.

All three components of phonological processing are important for speech production as well as the development of the spoken and written language skills necessary for reading.

Example Question

An ELL is struggling to identify certain sounds in words. What would be the best approach to help the student develop phonemic awareness?

    A. Determine if the student has phonemic awareness in the first language.

    B. Have the student work with an English learner who is fluent in English.

    C. Require the student to use English only when speaking.

    D. Use pictures to help the student identify different words.

Correct Answer: A

The question is asking about phonemic awareness, which is skills focused on sounds only. Nurturing the student's first language so the student can master the skills in the second language is very important for ELLs. Answers B and C are not correct. Answer D is not effective in developing phonemic awareness. When answering questions about English learners, promoting the student's first language is often the correct answer.

English Syntax

There are four baseline rules to keep in mind when thinking about basic English syntax:

1. A complete sentence requires a subject and a verb and expresses a complete thought. This is also called an independent clause. A sentence without a subject and a verb is considered a fragment.

2. Separate ideas generally require separate sentences. A sentence containing multiple independent clauses that are improperly joined is considered a run-on sentence.

3. English word order follows the subject-verb-object sequence. (It's usually the same in French and Spanish.)

4. A dependent clause contains a subject and a verb—but it doesn't express a complete thought.

On the ESOL/ESL exam, you will be required to understand basic concepts of grammar and how to teach them effectively.

Parts of Speech

Part of Speech	Description	Example
Noun	person, place or thing	car, boat, pilot, rock
Pronoun	replaces a noun	it, he, she, him/her, they, them
Verb	action words	run, walk, shop, talk
Adjective	describes nouns	pretty, exciting, small, big
Adverb	modifies verbs, adjectives, or other adverbs	slowly, quickly, well, pleasantly
Preposition	word placed before a noun or pronoun to form a phrase modifying another word	by, over, under, with, for
Conjunction	words that join clauses or phrases	for, and, nor, but, or, yet, so (FANBOYS)
Interjection	words that express emotion	Oh! Wow! Yikes!

Quick Tip

Modal verbs are verbs that link other verbs. Modal verbs are auxiliary verbs (also called helping verbs) like **can, will, could, shall, must, would, might, and should**. Modal verbs add meaning to the main verb in a sentence by expressing possibility, ability, permission, or obligation.

For example:

She <u>must complete</u> her homework before playing outside.

Clause - a unit of grammatical organization consisting of a subject and predicate

Example

Which of the following is considered a clause?

    A. Walking down the street

    B. While they were on their way to school

    C. The girl from Ohio

    D. The teacher and the students

Correct Answer: B

Notice in answer B, if you take away the word *while*, you have the clause *they were on their way to school*. That has a subject and a predicate. None of the other answer choices do.

Identifying independent and dependent clauses

The best approach to this part of the assessment is to understand the difference between independent clauses and dependent clauses.

- An **independent clause** contains a subject and a verb and expresses a complete thought. An independent clause can stand on its own as a sentence.

- A **dependent clause** contains a noun and a verb but does not express a complete thought. A dependent clause cannot be a sentence on its own.

Example:

Fragments

Dependent clauses, without the independent clause in a sentence, are fragments. Fragments are not sentences.

Incorrect:

Correct:

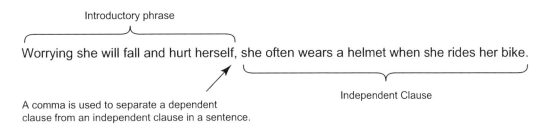

Introductory phrase

Worrying she will fall and hurt herself, she often wears a helmet when she rides her bike.

Independent Clause

A comma is used to separate a dependent clause from an independent clause in a sentence.

Quick Tip

You can take a fragment and add it to an independent clause to make a complete sentence as long as you place a comma, separating them appropriately.

Example question

Choose the option that corrects an error in the underlined portion(s). If no error exists, choose "No change is necessary."

She is constantly checking her <u>work. Making</u> sure she didn't make any mistakes.

   A. work, making

   B. work; making

   C. work making

   D. No change is necessary.

Correct answer: A

Think Like a Test Maker

Remember, ELLs learn grammar in a natural order. For example, students learn simple sentences first, then compound sentences, then complex sentences. This aligns with Krashen's Natural Order Hypothesis, discussed later in the study guide.

In this case, *Making sure she didn't make any mistakes* is a fragment; it is just the verb phrase. Therefore, it cannot be a sentence on its own as it is originally presented, making option D "No change is necessary" incorrect. In answer choice B, the semicolon is incorrect because semicolons separate two independent clauses. The clause *Making sure she didn't make any mistakes* is not an independent clause. Having no punctuation between the two clauses makes the sentence a run-on and, therefore, incorrect, eliminating answer choice C. In answer choice A, a comma between *work* and *making* is correct because the comma is separating an independent clause from a dependent clause.

Sentence Type	Explanation	Example
Simple sentence	Consists of one **independent** clause	I went to the store.
Compound sentence	Consists of **two independent** clauses. Ensure that there is a comma between two independent clauses in a compound sentence. The comma should be followed by a coordinating conjunction (**FANBOYS**).	I went to the store, and I bought milk.
Complex sentence	Consists of an independent clause and a dependent clause. When the sentence starts with a dependent clause, a comma is needed after the clause.	When I went to the store, I bought milk.
Compound complex sentence	Consists of at least two independent clauses and at least one dependent clause.	When I went to the store, I bought milk, and I bought cheese.

In addition to types of sentences, ELLs will struggle with tense when they speak. Below is a chart of the different types of tenses in the English Language,

Verb Tense	Past	Present	Future
Simple	He walked down the street.	He walks down the street.	He will walk down the street.
Continuous	He was walking down the street.	He is walking down the street.	He will be walking down the street.
Perfect	He had walked down the street.	He has walked down the street.	He will have six credits by the end of the semester.
Perfect continuous	He had been walking down the street.	He has been walking down the street.	He will have been in school for five years by next Tuesday.

Interrogative and Relative Pronouns

These are called interrogative pronouns because they are used to ask questions—an interrogative sentence asks a question.

- Who is going to the dance?
- With whom is she going to the dance?
- Whoever thought the dance would be this exciting?

Just like with regular pronouns—he/him/his, she/her/hers, we/us/ours, etc.—who, whom, and whose belong in certain parts of the sentence.

Subject Pronouns - They occur in the subject part of the sentence.	Object Pronouns – They occur in the prepositional phrase or in the predicate part of a sentence.	Possessive Pronouns – They show possession in the sentence.
who/whoever	whom/whomever	whose
Who went to the store? **Who** won the game? **Whoever** thought this would happen? **Whoever** decided to do that was wrong.	To **whom** are you speaking? He had a date with **whom**? That is the man with **whom** my father used to live. You can go with **whomever** you want.	**Whose** car is this? This is the lady **whose** generous funding created this scholarship.

The writing Process

Be sure to understand the main modes of writing.

Opinion/argumentative – Writing that persuades or convinces using support, details, and examples from the text in logical order. In early grades, this is called *opinion writing*.

Informative/explanatory – Writing that informs, explains, or tells "how to" without using opinions (just the facts).

Descriptive – Writing that describes or helps form a visual picture using sensory details and spatial order.

Narrative – A first-person account that tells a story as it happens using sensory details and chronological order.

Writing clearly and coherently is challenging for most students, but particularly for students whose first language is not English. Therefore, teachers must provide students with tools to help with the writing process. There are several ways teachers can help students write clearly and coherently.

- **Organization** – It is important that students organize their writing by first mapping what they are going to write. Mind maps and other graphic organizers can help students do this.

- **Transitional words** – These words connect parts of a paragraph to one another. Helping students identify the right transitional words is useful in coherent writing.

- **Cooperative learning** – These writing workshops help students revise their writing. Peer reviews, brainstorming sessions, and editing roundtables can help students revise their writing in an effective manner. It is important to remember that for cooperative learning to be effective, it must be organized, and everyone in the group must have a role.

- **Frameworks** – These formulas allow students to follow a step-by-step structure as they write. This allows students to plug their information into the pre-established formula. As the students get more proficient in writing, they can modify or abandon the formula.

- **Rubrics** – These assessment tools outline expectations for student writing. Students should not have to guess what the teacher wants to see in the writing assignment. Rubrics outline a set of parameters that help students focus their writing.

Stages of the Writing Process

- **Pre-writing** – Brainstorming, considering purpose and goals for writing, using graphic organizers
- **Drafting** – Working independently to draft the sentence, essay, or paper
- **Peer review** – Students evaluate each other's writing in the peer review process
- **Revising** – Reworking a piece of writing based on structure, tone, and clear connections
- **Editing** – Editing based on conventions and mechanics
- **Rewriting** – Incorporating changes as they carefully write or type their final drafts
- **Publishing** – Producing and disseminating the work in a variety of ways, such as a class book, bulletin board, letters to the editor, school newsletter, or website

Demonstrate the reciprocity of decoding and encoding

Decoding involves translating printed words to sounds or reading. Encoding is the opposite: using individual sounds to build and write words.

Ways to teach decoding:

- Have students sound out individual sounds in words they see in print.
- Have students segment words based on sounds or chunks.
- Have students use onset and rime to decode words.

Ways to teach encoding:

- Have students use phonetic spelling to translate words.
- Engage in regular spelling tests.
- Have student write down words they recognize.

Think Like a Test Maker

Decoding and encoding are interrelated and are essential in building students' phonics skills.

1. Students in an 8th grade class are analyzing the different sounds in Spanish and in English. They notice that the different sounds in words have nothing to do with meaning. The sounds are simply ways in which different cultures produce words. This concept aligns with which of the following:

   A. Language is rule-governed

   B. Language is systematic

   C. Language is arbitrary

   D. Language is morphology

2. Two ELLs are working on their L2 development. They are using spelling and phonics to understand words. What principle of universal language are they using?

   A. Rule-governed

   B. Systematic

   C. Arbitrary

   D. Morphology

3. A teacher is going over the past-tense and present-tense verbs during language instruction. Which of the following principles of universal language is the teacher focusing on?

   A. Language is rule-governed

   B. Language is systematic

   C. Language is arbitrary

   D. Language is morphology

4. ELLs in a 4th grade class are using sounds in words and working on their letter to sound relationships. They are working on:

   A. Vocabulary

   B. Morphology

   C. Grammar

   D. Phonology

5. During a fluency read, an advanced ESOL student is reading aloud to the teacher. When the student gets to a difficult word, she uses the words around the difficult word to figure out its meaning. This student is using what type of cueing system?

   A. Syntactic

   B. Semantic

   C. Graphophonic

   D. Pragmatic

Foundation of Linguistics

6. Students are reading through a piece of text. When they get to difficult words or phrases, the teacher asks, "Does that fit the social setting in this situation?" The teacher is helping students to use which cueing system?

   A. Semantic

   B. Syntactic

   C. Graphophonic

   D. Pragmatic

7. Students are breaking apart compound words like "sidewalk" and "rattlesnake" to figure out their meaning. They are also analyzing how the prefix "un" means "no" or "not." These students are using:

   A. Phonology

   B. Pragmatics

   C. Morphology

   D. Grammar

8. A teacher wants students to summarize the key events in a story. She has them use L2 in cooperative groups to discuss the story. The teacher is using which linguistic method?

   A. Syntactic analysis

   B. Discourse in context

   C. Group work

   D. Morphemic

9. Which of the following would be the most effective way to help students increase their L2 exposure and fluency?

   A. Provide opportunities for students to use language in context.

   B. Regularly test students on their language application in class.

   C. Provide students with at-home practice to sharpen their skills.

   D. Require students to only speak the second language when at school.

10. When reading aloud, an ELL replaces the *ph* (*f* sound) with a /p/ /h/ sound. What miscue is the student experiencing?

    A. Semantic

    B. Syntactic

    C. Graphophonic

    D. Pragmatic

Number	Answer	Explanation
1.	C	**Language is rule-governed** – Most languages are governed by grammar where there are patterns and rules the language follows. **Language is systematic** – This is the letter to sound relationship in words. This is known as phonics (spelling) in English. **Language is arbitrary** – The sounds in language have nothing to do with meaning. They are essentially random sounds cultures use to make words. **Language is morphology** – This is the nonsense answer. Morphology is the study of word parts based on individual word meanings.
2.	B	Think of it this way: **Rule-governed** = grammar **Systematic** = phonics **Arbitrary** = random **Morphology** is the smallest units of meaning in a word. Prefixes, suffixes, roots, and compound words are typically used in morphology questions.
3.	A	A lesson on past tense and present tense verbs is a lesson in grammar. Grammar has to do with rule-governed language. **Language is rule-governed** – Most languages are governed by grammar where there are patterns and rules the language follows. **Language is systematic** – This is the letter to sound relationship in words. This is known as phonics (spelling) in English. **Language is arbitrary** – The sounds in language have nothing to do with meaning. They are essentially random sounds cultures use to make words. **Language is morphology** – This is the nonsense answer. Morphology is the study of word parts based on individual word meanings.
4.	D	The root word *phon* means sound. Phonology is the study of sound to letter relationships.
5.	B	When students use meaning to figure out words, they are using semantics. Syntactic cues are grammar and structure cues. Graphophonic or phonics are spelling cues, and pragmatics are social cues.
6.	D	The keywords in this question are *social setting*. When students use social norms to figure out the proper word, they are using pragmatics.
7.	C	Morphology is the study of the smallest meanings in words. In this scenario, students are using the smallest parts of words to derive meaning. Whenever students are using compound words or prefixes, suffixes and roots, they are using morphology.

Number	Answer	Explanation
8.	B	Because students are engaging in a conversation, they are using context and discourse. *In context* is another way of saying real-world or relevant. In this case, a conversation is a real-world application of the new language.
9.	A	Typically, the most effective way to build fluency in a new language is to use it in context. Avoid answer choices like B, C, and D on this exam.
10.	C	Remember, graphophonic refers to letter-sound relationships. In this case, she is not applying the *ph* rule (phonics) to the word.

Foundation
of Linguistics

III – Foundations of Language Acquisition

One of the most important concepts to remember when teaching ELLs is that teachers must always support L1 in order to develop L2. The goal is NOT to replace L1. The goal is to strengthen L1 to support L2 development.

Communicative Competence

In terms of teaching ELLs, teachers must use techniques to strengthen communicative competence. Communicative competence is the ability of second language learners to apply and use language appropriately. Communicative competence has four stages:

1. **Grammatical** – understanding of syntax, morphology, and foundational skills (phonology in the second language)

2. **Social linguistics** – the rules of discourse. For example, formality, politeness, idioms, expressions, and background knowledge

   - **Register** is formal vs informal discourse. For example, if a student says to the teacher, "Give me that piece of paper," the student may not know that she is making an error in register because she is speaking too informally to the teacher. Instead, the student should say, "May I please have that piece of paper," or "Please hand me that paper."

3. **Discourse** – understanding that ideas are connected through patterns, conjunctions (and, but, so), sequentially, and by importance

4. **Strategic** – techniques that overcome language gaps. For example, modifying communication based on the audience and purpose

An important part of communicative competence is helping students think critically.

Krashen's Theory of Second Language Acquisition

A large part of how teachers instruct ELLs is through an understanding of Krashen's Theory of second language acquisition. Krashen's theory of second language acquisition consists of five main hypotheses:

1. **Acquisition-learning hypothesis** – According to Krashen (1981), there are two distinct systems in the acquisition learning hypothesis: the acquired system and the learned system.

   - **Acquired system** is the product of a subconscious process similar to what children undergo when they acquire their first language. It requires meaningful interaction or natural communication language. This is an *inductive* approach and is usually student-centered. Therefore, roleplay can be an effective tool for teaching students a second language.

   - **Learned system** is the product of formal instruction that requires a conscious process. For example, understanding grammar rules in the second language is part of the learned system. This approach is *deductive* and usually teacher-centered.

Quick Tip

Inductive reasoning is based on observation. For example, when ELLs are learning conversational English, they are observing their peers and emulating what they do.

Deductive reasoning is based on widely recognized rules. For example, when ELLs are learning to read, they are using widely recognized English phonics rules to sound out and recognize words.

2. **Monitor hypothesis** – Think of this as the editor inside the ELL's brain monitoring speaking and listening. The monitoring function is the practical result of the learned grammar. The monitor acts, plans, edits, and corrects as long as the ELL has met three conditions:

   1. The second language learner has sufficient time at their disposal.

   2. They focus on form or think about correctness.

   3. They know the rule.

3. **Input hypothesis** – This is how language acquisition takes place. The learner improves and progresses along the *natural order* when he/she receives second language 'input' that is one step beyond his/her current stage of linguistic competence.

   Think Like a Test Maker

   When the affective filter is high, students can feel unmotivated, intimidated, and uneasy. When the affective filter is low, students feel safe and encouraged to try and task risks. Therefore, teachers should work to *lower* the affective filter.

   • **Comprehensible input** highlights that students learn best when they take in information in a low-anxiety environment. According to Krashen (1981), language acquisition requires meaningful interaction in the target language,

4. **Affective filter hypothesis** – These variables include motivation, self-confidence, anxiety, and personality traits. Krashen claims that learners with high motivation, self-confidence, a good self-image, and a low level of anxiety have a high chance of success in second language acquisition. Low motivation, low self-esteem, high anxiety, introversion, and inhibition can raise the affective filter and form a 'mental block' that prevents comprehensible input from being used for acquisition. Therefore, it is very important to make the classroom a safe place where students are motivated to try new things in terms of language acquisition.

5. **Natural order hypothesis** - The acquisition of grammatical structures follows a 'natural order' which is predictable in all languages. For example, students learn the present tense before they can understand past tense.

Communication strategies

Often when an ELL is speaking or trying to communicate with teachers and peers, the student will use communication strategies. The following are a few examples:

   • **Code switching** – switching from L2 to L1 when the student does not have the words to express what the student is saying. The following is an example.

   Teacher: Tell me about your time at the beach this weekend.

   Student: It was fun, but I don't like it that much because of the, how do you say, *arena* (sand). It gets on everything, and I don't like it.

   In this example, the student code switches by using the Spanish word when he does not know the English word for sand.

   • **Language convergence** – linguistic changes in which languages come to resemble one another because of continued language contact and mutual interference. An example of this is how Portuguese and Spanish have many similar characteristics.

   • **Language interference** – When L1 interferes with L2. For example, in Spanish, adjectives come after the nouns (la playa bonita – beach pretty). In English, adjectives come before the noun (pretty beach). When students are learning a new language, their first language syntax can interfere with the new syntax. A student might say, "It was a beach very pretty."

- **Context vs explicit** – Context is learning based on other meanings around the word or sentence. Explicit is learning based on a set of rules.

- **Lexical approach** – the assumption that language consists of meaningful chunks when combined to produce fluent, clear speech.

- **Back-channeling** – Utterances from the listener that indicate understanding. In English, back-channeling usually takes the form of utterances such as *uh-huh, yeah, mmm, okay, right, wow!, really?*

- **Self-repair** – When a speaker fixes an error in language. For example, and ELL is reading history and says, "The people were unable to go to school. They were *depressed*. I mean *oppressed*."

Students with Limited or Interrupted Formal Education (SLIFE)

Sometimes students who come from other countries have interruptions in their formal education in their first language. For example, a student who is the age of a third grader in the U.S. may have had a year or more when he or she did not go to school because of several reasons. This is particularly challenging for the teacher and student.

Think about it!

ELLs are not a monolith (consisting of only one type of person or belief). ELLs are high-achieving, gifted, autistic, exceptional, advanced, at risk, and more.

Some students will come from backgrounds where they had extensive formal education, and others will have little formal education.

Therefore, it is imperative that ESOL teachers differentiate to meet the needs of every student.

Activities to Promote Language Acquisition

Cloze Activity

These are activities where students fill in the blanks in a short reading passage. To test their comprehension and understanding of a text, students must fill in the missing words. Cloze activities can be created using any text, including poems, songs, and non-fiction pieces. Some cloze activities only have a few blanks, while more difficult cloze activities have many blanks. In fact, a teacher can create multiple cloze activities from the same text. Finally, some cloze activities include a word bank students can use for further assistance.

Total Physical Response (TPR)

This is a method of teaching language or vocabulary concepts by using physical movement to react to verbal input. The process mimics the way that infants learn their first language, and it reduces student inhibitions and lowers stress. An example of this is using the activity *Head, Shoulders, Knees, and Toes* in physical education class. Another example is following a recipe as the teacher demonstrates in culinary class.

Quick Tip

In second language acquisition (SLA) research, the critical period is the ideal time period to acquire language in a linguistically rich environment. After the critical period, it is thought that SLA becomes more difficult and requires a greater amount of effort.

Language Experience Approach (LEA)

The language experience approach (LEA) is a literacy development method that has been used for early reading development with ELLs. This approach combines all four language skills: listening, speaking, reading, and writing.

Foundations of Language Acquisition

This page intentionally left blank.

1. A 6th grade teacher has several ELLs in class who have had interruptions in their formal education in L1. What would be the most appropriate way to approach activities with these students in the beginning of the year or during their beginning lessons?

   A. Have the students read aloud for practice.

   B. Introduce commonly used words across contexts.

   C. Assign extra homework so they can make up time lost.

   D. Focus primarily on grammar rules.

2. A student says, "I was excited for school today. I have my books and...*lapices.* I got new shoes too." In this instance, the student does not know the English word for pencils, so the student uses the Spanish word *lapices.* This is an example of:

   A. Assimilation

   B. Acculturation

   C. Code switching

   D. Affect filter

3. A student is using grammar concepts in L1 to learn grammar concepts in L2. This is called:

   A. Translation

   B. Negative transfer

   C. Positive transfer

   D. Semantic transfer

4. Which of the following is usually true about second language acquisition?

   A. Students who receive support in L1 while learning L2 do better at acquiring L2 than those who do not receive support in L1.

   B. Students who receive little support in L1 while learning L2 do better at acquiring L2 than those who receive too much support in L1.

   C. Students who are completely immersed in L2 and engage in English-only practices in the classroom acquire L2 more quickly than those who use L1 and L2.

   D. Students who want to be proficient in a second language should replace L1 with L2 as soon as possible.

5. Julia is an ELL who is proficient in L1 and L2 but struggles with informational, academic text in L2. The class is working on a research paper and will need to evaluate lots of informational text. What can the teacher do to support Julia during this process?

   A. Require Julia to do the research and present in English but allow her to use a Spanish to English dictionary.

   B. Have Julia work with a partner who is more proficient in L2 during the research process and allow Julia to present in L1.

   C. Reduce the number of pages Julia has to read for the research paper and allow her to present in L2.

   D. Allow Julia to conduct the research in L1 when she needs to and have her present her findings in English.

6. A sixth-grade teacher is helping students get excited about learning English and even implements games to make learning English fun. The teacher's goal is to increase motivation. The teacher is working on what part of the theory of language acquisition?

   A. Natural order hypothesis

   B. Affective filter hypothesis

   C. Input hypothesis

   D. Monitor hypothesis

Use the following scenario to answer questions 7-10.

As part of an informal assessment of ELLs' writing skills in English, an ESL teacher has the students write short narratives about shopping at the grocery store. A sample of student narratives are as follows:

   • It was a store very big.

   • My mother found el pollo fresh.

   • We also got fruits and vegetables for la cena (dinner).

7. The teacher can determine that the type of interference occurring in this student's communication is:

   A. Syntax

   B. Phonics

   C. Pragmatics

   D. Phonemic awareness

8. Which of the following activities would be beneficial in helping the student correct this error?

   A. Spelling instruction

   B. Role play

   C. Diagramming sentences

   D. Vocab instruction

9. Which of the following interference conditions is happening in the third sentence of the student's narrative?

   A. Pragmatics

   B. Code switching

   C. Social linguistics

   D. Syntax

10. Which of the following would be most beneficial to help this ELL fix the errors in his narrative?

   A. Have the student do extra homework in the areas he is low.

   B. Have the student work with a peer to correct the issues in his narrative.

   C. Give the student extra practice in grammar.

   D. Provide the student with specific and meaningful feedback.

Number	Answer	Explanation
1.	B	Answer B is most appropriate and most effective because it helps to activate the student's background knowledge.
2.	C	The student is switching to Spanish words when the student cannot remember the words in English. This is code switching.
3.	C	This is considered positive transfer because the skills from L1 are helping in L2. Sometimes concepts in L1 can impede concepts in L2 and cause confusion. In that case, it is negative transfer. Answers A and D are nonsense answers.
4.	A	Bilingual education is key. The research shows that students who receive support in their first language (L1) will do better in acquiring their second language (L2). All of the other answer choices are bad practice when teaching ELLs.
5.	D	In this case, the teacher scaffolds the research process for Julia while keeping standards high. The teacher is also supporting L1 and L2 in this situation. All the other answer choices reduce the standards or do not support Julia in L1. Julia is proficient in L2 except for academic reading. Therefore, she should present in L2.
6.	B	The affective filter is about students' feelings and motivation (Krashen, 1981).
7.	A	The student is putting the adjectives after the nouns, which is correct in Spanish but not in English. This is an error in syntax or English grammar.
8.	C	By diagramming sentences, the student will be able to identify where the adjectives go in the sentence.
9.	B	The student does not know the name for dinner, so the student code switches and uses the Spanish term—cena.
10.	D	Specific and meaningful feedback is essential so students can understand what they did incorrectly and are able to fix it.

Foundations of Language Acquisition

This page intentionally left blank.

IV – Cultural Awareness

IMPORTANT - One of the most important parts of being culturally aware and culturally responsive is understanding that language and culture are interrelated. Be sure to keep that in mind when teaching and while taking this exam.

Cultural Variables in Language Acquisition

Rossi-Landi (1973) asserts that children learn their language from their societies, and during the process of learning a language also learn their culture and develop their cognitive abilities. Learning a language is therefore learning the behavior of a given society and its cultural customs.

Student identity – It is important that ESOL teachers respect students' identities as students begin to learn English. Many students will want to fit in and even want to leave behind their culture. Teachers must find a way to celebrate students' identities, cultures, and differences while helping them learn English.

Bias – A prejudice in favor of or against one thing, person, or group compared with another, usually in a way considered to be unfair. Teachers must be aware of their implicit bias.

- **Implicit bias** – An unconscious association, belief, or attitude toward any cultural or social group. Due to implicit biases, people may often attribute certain qualities or characteristics to all members of a particular group, a phenomenon known as stereotyping (Cherry, 2020). This can hinder a teacher's objectivity when teaching ELLs.

- **Stereotyping** – Studies have also demonstrated that implicit bias can have a negative impact on educational access and academic achievement of culturally diverse students (Cherry, 2020).

- **Ethnocentrism** – To use one's own culture or ethnicity as a frame of reference to judge other cultures, and people, rather than using the standards of the culture involved.

Respect for cultural and linguistic diversity

It is important that ESOL teachers remember that ELLs are not a monolith and that students are struggling with biculturalism (speaking one language and being one way at school and speaking another language and being another way at home).

- **Acculturation** – This is the cultural modification of an individual, group, or people by adapting to or borrowing traits from another culture. It is a merging of cultures because of prolonged contact.

- **Assimilation** – This is when two cultures compete, and the minority culture is abandoned. This should NOT be the goal.

- **Enculturation** – This is the process by which an individual learns the traditional content of a culture and assimilates its practices and values

- **Additive Bilingualism** – This learning the second language without replacing or dropping the first language and culture.

Think Like a Test Maker

Two-way immersion programs are designed to integrate native-speaking English speakers and ELLs in the same classroom with the goal of academic excellence and bilingual proficiency for both groups. Therefore, one feature of a two-way immersion program is to promote additive bilingualism.

Cultural variables in language acquisition

Sociolinguistics is concerned with language in social and cultural context, specifically how people with varying social identities, such as race, ethnicity, and class, speak and how their speech changes in different situations. Sociolinguistics is also defined by how language and culture are interrelated in terms of habits, customs, and needs of a community.

Celebrating Culture

When teaching in diverse classrooms, celebrating culture and integrating culturally responsive practices should be ongoing.

Home language supports are practices effective teachers use to support ELLs. Sending information home in the students' home languages is very important. Allowing students to speak in their home language when they need to do so is also important. A bilingual approach is most effective when helping students learn English. "English only" practices should be avoided in the classroom and eliminated as answer choices on the exam.

Family involvement

Involving families is imperative in students' success. This does not mean only calling the parents when their student misbehaves. Rather, authentic family involvement includes continually connecting with parents to include them in the school community through events such as family nights, student-led conferences, and newsletters (in the home language). Having students personally invite their parents to student-led conferences or school events is also very effective in getting parents and guardians involved. The school should provide interpreters for school events, conferences, and due process hearings.

Multi-Tiered Systems of Support (MTSS)

The MTSS framework is evidence-based and has had a significant impact on addressing the needs of different subgroups of students (Gordillo, 2015). MTSS can be an effective approach for ELLs who struggle.

- MTSS addresses academic as well as the social, emotional, and behavioral development of children from early childhood to graduation (Hurst, 2014).

- MTSS provides multiple levels of support for all learners—struggling through advanced (Hurst, 2014).

MTSS Tiered Systems	
Tier I	Modifications or differentiated instruction **all** students get in the form of instruction (academic and behavior/social-emotional) and student supports. Tier I is the basic and general implementation of the core curriculum that is aligned to the state standards.
Tier II	Modifications or differentiated instruction **some** students receive in addition to Tier I instruction. Tier II instruction and supports improve student performance under Tier I performance expectations. This is also referred to as accommodations. The standards and expectations remain the same as Tier I. However, additional accommodations are used for these students to be successful.
Tier III	Modifications or differentiated instruction **few** students receive and the most intense service level a school can provide to a student. Typically, Tier III services are provided to very small groups and/or individual students. Tier III services help students overcome significant barriers to learning academic and/or behavior skills required for school success.

Think Like a Test Maker

The **notional-functional** approach in ESL or ESOL instruction is a way of designing classroom instruction and materials around *notions* or real-life situations. This includes the way people communicate Then these *notions* are further broken down into *functions* or specific ways of communication. This helps ELLs acquire knowledge necessary to communicate effectively. It is important that teachers are culturally aware when implementing these practices.

Cultural Awareness

This page intentionally left blank.

IV – Cultural Awareness Practice Questions

1. When ELLs adopt American culture, abandon their native culture, and speak English at school, at home, and with friends, they are in what stage of cultural adaptation?

   A. Multiculturalism

   B. Socialization

   C. Acculturation

   D. Assimilation

2. Rosa lives in the United States and teaches at the local university. She speaks English at work and has many American colleagues and friends. She also maintains relationships with people from her culture with whom she regularly speaks her home language and maintains her first culture. Rosa is displaying what type of cultural adaptation?

   A. Multiculturalism

   B. Socialization

   C. Acculturation

   D. Assimilation

3. A new teacher has several ELLs in class. The teacher notices that they are not participating as much as the other students and wants to motivate them to engage. What would be the most effective way to engage these students?

   A. Call home and ask their parents to speak with the students.

   B. Design relevant lessons and activities aligned with the students' interests.

   C. Continue doing the same thing and allow the students to engage when ready.

   D. Separate the students so they are working with English speakers only.

4. Ms. Jones is a teacher at a school with a large ELL population. What can she do to be sure she is being culturally sensitive to her students?

   A. Design activities that promote critical thinking and are aligned to the academic standards.

   B. Continually praise her ELLs for making strides in reading and writing.

   C. Implement a system of rewards for students when they reach their learning goals.

   D. Encourage students to work in groups and help each other learn.

5. A new ELL has enrolled in the school. She keeps to herself and is quiet in class. What would be the most appropriate approach to take with this student?

   A. Introduce the student to the class and have her partner up with a fluent English speaker.

   B. Meet with the student privately and allow the student to engage when ready.

   C. Call home and ask her parents to encourage her to engage in class.

   D. Have the student work alone with a translator until she is ready to join class.

Cultural Awareness

6. In a culturally and linguistically diverse class, what can a teacher do to ensure students are receiving a culturally responsive education?

    A. Design curriculum and instruction that integrates language and culture.

    B. Insist that students immerse themselves completely in the new language.

    C. Communicate with parents for an at-home plan to support the classroom.

    D. Choose lessons that are easily transferred to the first language.

7. Learning a new culture's behaviors, expectations, and norms through interacting with the teacher and other students is called:

    A. Acculturation

    B. Assimilation

    C. Enculturation

    D. Socialization

8. What is the most effective way to teach ELLs in a social science class?

    A. Immerse students completely in L2 and only allow them to speak L2 during academic time.

    B. Have students speak L2 socially in groups and then move to academic vocabulary.

    C. Make connections between L1 and L2, focusing on L2 while scaffolding to support L1.

    D. Create engaging lessons to support L2 acquisition as soon as possible.

9. Which of the following would be the most effective way to communicate to students and parents about upcoming classroom events and deadlines?

    A. A well-maintained teacher website where students and parents can access information regularly

    B. Colorful posters in the classroom that display important information for the semester

    C. Weekly emails sent to every parent and student

    D. A detailed monthly newsletter sent home with students in the students' home languages

10. Mr. Sunni will be starting a lesson on Native American poetry. He knows some of the language and concepts will be challenging for students. What can he do at the beginning of the lesson to help students grasp difficult concepts presented in the poetry?

    A. Allow students to use the Internet to search confusing concepts.

    B. Have students create a word list of confusing words they will look up after the lesson.

    C. Have a guest speaker come in and talk to the students about Native American culture.

    D. Help students activate their prior knowledge to understand complex concepts.

Think Like a Test Maker

Number	Answer	Explanation
1.	D	When two cultures compete, the minority culture is abandoned, and the dominant culture is adopted, it is called assimilation.
2.	C	Acculturation is when a person adopts the dominant culture for school and work while maintaining the first language and culture at home and with family.
3.	B	To motivate students to learn, whether they are ELL or native speakers, relevance and interest is crucial. These are considered good words to look for in the correct answer choices on this exam.
4.	A	Promoting critical thinking in the classroom means the teacher has high expectations for all students. Also, state standards are essential in lesson planning and instruction. If you see *aligned to the state standards* in the answer choices, it is most likely the correct answer. While praise and rewards are okay to use in the classroom, they are associated with extrinsic motivators. Extrinsic motivators are often not the correct answer on the exam.
5.	B	This student is probably experiencing culture shock. Forcing the student to engage or introducing the student to the class could exacerbate the culture shock. The best thing to do is let the student know you are there for support and allow the student to engage when ready.
6.	A	Effective ESOL teachers understand that language and culture are interrelated, and both must be considered when designing curriculum and instruction. Answers B, C, and D are typically not the correct answers on this exam.
7.	C	**Enculturation** is the process by which an individual learns the culture that they are surrounded by. It enables them to function as members of that society. **Acculturation** is when a person adopts the dominant culture for school and work while maintaining the first language and culture. **Assimilation** is when two cultures compete, the minority culture is abandoned, and the dominant culture is adopted. **Socialization** is when students self-advocate, ask questions, and develop healthy relationships.
8.	C	Answer choice C outlines bilingual education, which is most effective because it focuses on L2 acquisition, but it also includes supports in L1. This helps students draw connections from L1 to L2.
9.	D	Always send home with students a physical copy in the students' home languages. This is an example of being culturally responsive. Whenever communicating important events or deadlines, it is important teachers remember that not all students have Internet access; this eliminates answers A and D. Colorful posters are not effective in notifying parents about important events and deadlines.
10.	D	Activating prior knowledge is essential in drawing connections from the text to self. Helping students use their prior experiences and understanding to learn new concepts is effective.

Cultural Awareness

This page intentionally left blank.

V – Assessment

Effective teachers select the most appropriate assessment at the appropriate time to measure the appropriate skills. You will be required to understand different assessments. Remember, assessments should *always be used to make instructional decisions*.

Assessment Type	Definition	Example
Diagnostic	A pre-assessment providing instructors with information about students' prior knowledge, preconceptions, and misconceptions before beginning a learning activity.	Before starting a reading unit on Earth space science, a teacher gives a quick assessment to determine students' prior knowledge of concepts in the text. She uses this information to make instructional decisions moving forward.
Formative	A range of formal and informal assessments or checks conducted by the teacher before, during, and after the learning process in order to modify instruction.	A teacher walks around the room checking on students as they read. She might also write anecdotal notes to review later to help her design further instruction.
Summative	An assessment that focuses on the outcomes. It is frequently used to measure the effectiveness of a program, lesson, or strategy.	A reading teacher gives a mid-term exam at the end of the semester to measure students' mastery of standards.
Performance-Based	An assessment that measures students' ability to apply the skills and knowledge learned from a unit or units of study. These assessments challenge students to use their higher-order, critical thinking skills to create a product or complete a process.	After reading text about the Civil War, students develop stories about different historical figures in the war. Students then perform these stories in front of the class and answer questions.
Criterion-Referenced	An assessment that measures student performance against a fixed set of predetermined criteria or learning standards.	At the end of the spring semester, students take the state standardized reading assessment. The state uses the scores for accountability measures.
Norm-Referenced (Percentile)	An assessment or evaluation that yields an estimate of the position of the tested individual in a predefined population with respect to the trait being measured.	The NAEP is an exam given every few years for data purposes only to compare students' reading scores across the U.S.
Universal Screening/ Placement Tests	An assessment used to place students in appropriate classrooms or grade level.	Students are typically screened throughout the year to determine at what level they are reading. Placement decisions are made based on the outcomes of the screening.

Major ESOL and ESL Assessments

English language proficiency (ELP) assessments are used to measure students' reading, writing, speaking, and listening skills defined in states' English language proficiency standards.

ELP assessments have two main purposes:

1. For a district or school to help identify ELLs who are eligible for services and those who can exit from services.

2. For states to annually track the English proficiency of students already identified as ELLs and to include the percentage of English learners reaching proficiency each year for Elementary and Secondary Education Act (ESEA) accountability. State assessments measure whether English learners attain English proficiency so that they have the opportunity to meet the same challenging content achievement standards as their peers.

Oral Assessments

Oral assessments are a way for teachers to check for understanding. Oral assessments include having students engage in:

- Retelling stories
- Roleplaying
- Giving descriptions or instructions using visual or written prompts
- Oral reporting to the whole class
- Telling a story by using a sequence of three or more pictures
- Completing dialogue or conversation through written prompts

Quick Tip

Oral assessments can measure comprehension, understanding, sequence, vocabulary, and more. They are also an effective way to differentiate assessments based on students' stages of language acquisition.

Alternative Assessments

- Formal and informal assessments to measure receptive and productive skills
- Portfolios
- Performance-based
- Project-based

Accommodations for state-mandated tests

Extra time is the most common assessment accommodations for ELLs. However, accommodations also include Spanish to English dictionaries, having the directions read in L1, and adapting testing environment and conditions.

Assessment issues

- **Validity** - the degree to which a test score can be interpreted and used for its intended purpose.

  Example: A test that is supposed to assess reading comprehension contains information that is confusing to students. Some of the content is culturally specific. Instead of reading, ELLs are trying to figure out some of the cultural nuances. In this case, the test's validity is in question because it is not testing students' reading comprehension; rather it is testing students' knowledge of a specific culture. To increase the test's validity, the teacher can use a neutral passage with little or no culturally specific content. This will ensure the skills being assessed are reading skills, which increase the test's validity.

- **Reliability** - the degree to which scores from a particular test are consistent from one use of the test to the next.

  Example: Students in first period took their unit test. Third period students experienced technical difficulty during their unit test because the Internet went down. In fifth period, there was a fire alarm that interrupted the test. Because the testing atmosphere varied from 1st, 3rd, and 5th period students, the reliability of the exam was compromised. This is one reason why all classrooms are set up the same and all testing experiences are consistent during state standardized assessments. Consistency ensures reliability.

- **Test bias** – test design, or the way results are interpreted and used, that systematically puts certain groups of students at a disadvantage from others. Test bias can negatively affect students of color, students from lower-income backgrounds, ELLs, or students who are not fluent in certain cultural customs and traditions (Glossary of Education Reform, 2015).

  Example: Students are given a reading test that contains lots of cultural nuances that are unfamiliar to them because they did not grow up in the U.S. The test is culturally biased in this situation.

- **Objective vs Subjective**

  - Objective exams – fill-in-the-blank, multiple choice, those that have definitive answers.

  - Subjective tests – essays, presentations, those that require a person to score the exams.

Think Like a Test Maker

Know the difference between *quantitative* and *qualitative* data. *Quantitative* data includes measures that *can* be quantified with numbers, like test scores, reading levels, and correct words per min. *Qualitative* measures are those that *cannot* be quantified with numbers. *Qualitative* measures include observations, anecdotal notes, surveys, discussions, conferences, and writing samples. Remember, using both *quantitative* and *qualitative* measures together will give you the most accurate measure of a student's abilities.

WIDA ACCESS for ELLs assessments

Currently, 41 states use WIDA assessments to measure ELLs' language skills before placing students in classes. These assessments include:

- Assessment of the four language domains of listening, speaking, reading, and writing.

- Alignment with the WIDA English Language development standards in Social and Instructional Language, Language of Language Arts, Language of Mathematics, Language of Science, and Language of Social Studies.

ACCESS for ELLs is the main assessment WIDA provides. It is available to WIDA Consortium member states (41 states). The test is administered to kindergarten through twelfth grade students who have been identified as English language learners (ELLs). Given every year, it monitors students' progress in English acquisition. The test is aligned to the WIDA standards and meets the U.S. federal requirements of Every Student Succeeds Act (ESSA) for monitoring and reporting ELLs' progress toward English language proficiency.

The WIDA ACCESS test rates students based on proficiency score and then assigns them a language proficiency level:

WIDA Proficiency Levels		
1.	Entering	Knows and uses some social English and minimal academic English with visual and graphic support
2.	Emerging	Knows and uses some social and academic English with visual and graphic supports
3.	Developing	Uses social English and some academic English with visual supports
4.	Expanding	Uses social English and some academic English
5.	Bridging	Uses social and academic English on grade level
6.	Reaching	Uses social and academic English at the highest level

Each state sets its own reclassification score that determines when a student tests out of ESL or ESOL and no longer needs ELL services. Typically, level 5 (bridging) is the level ELLs need to be to test out of ESOL classes.

Assessment

State Exams

ELLs are expected to participate in state exams in reading and math. However, ELLs in most states are usually given the accommodation of extended time. Extended time is the most common accommodation for ELLs regarding state exams.

Extended time includes time and a half or 50% extra time. Extended time in some states means any amount of time the student needs to finish the exam. Remember, education policy is left mostly to states. Therefore, different states have different accommodation guidelines when it comes to ELLs and state testing.

The four criteria to facilitate the inclusion of ELLs in accommodated assessments, as defined by Rivera et al. (2006). These are the considerations most states use when determining if ELLs receive accommodations.

1. **Language-related** - English language proficiency, students' native language proficiency, language program placement, and primary language of instruction

2. **Academic-related** - academic background in home language and performance on other tests

3. **Time-related** - the time in U.S. or English-speaking schools or time in the state's schools

4. **Opinion-related** - include parent or guardian opinion or permission and teacher observation and recommendations

Assessment

This page intentionally left blank.

1. A teacher notices that a student is struggling to read a certain part of the text. The teacher wants to understand what specific skill the student is lacking so the teacher can address it. What assessment type would be the most effective in this situation?

   A. Summative

   B. Criterion-referenced

   C. Norm-referenced

   D. Diagnostic

2. Which of the following is the most effective way to use a criterion-referenced assessment?

   A. To compare student performances

   B. To drive instructional decisions

   C. To measure student learning at the end of a lesson

   D. To decide where to place students for class ranking

3. A formative assessment is:

   A. Ongoing and used as a final grade for students

   B. Static and used as a preassessment

   C. Static and used to compare student performances

   D. Ongoing and used to determine how to move forward with teaching

4. Which of the following provides rich qualitative data regarding an ELL's interaction with complex text?

   A. diagnostic assessment

   B. student survey

   C. anecdotal observation record

   D. oral assessment

5. Which of the following is the most common standardized assessment accommodation for ELL students?

   A. Extended time

   B. Translated test questions

   C. Translated answer choices

   D. Spanish to English dictionary

Assessment

6. A teacher is measuring students' story sequencing skills by having them write the sequence of the story in a graphic organizer. One ELL cannot write in English yet. What can the teacher do to measure this student's skills?

   A. Have a paraprofessional write for the student.

   B. Use an oral assessment instead of a written assessment.

   C. Require the student to write in English.

   D. Have another student write for the ELL student.

7. Ms. Rodrigues has several ELLs who have learning disabilities. What is the most effective way to meet the needs of these students?

   A. Call home and tell parents she will help them in any way she can.

   B. Reduce the amount of work she requires for the students with disabilities.

   C. Read and follow students' IEPs and align instruction to academic standards.

   D. Allow students extra time on assignments and tests.

8. Mr. Jackson is a new teacher with several ELLs in his English language arts class. When he assigns reading and comprehension questions, he notices that the students do not finish their work. What can he do to help these students?

   A. Have them tested for learning disabilities and suggest they receive IEPs.

   B. Have them sit in the front of the room so he can make sure they are doing their work.

   C. Call home and let the students' parents know that they are not finishing assignments.

   D. Use a diagnostic test to determine L2 ability and scaffold instruction accordingly.

9. When assessing a student's English language skills, what is the most important thing to consider?

   A. The student's proficiency level in the home language

   B. The education level of student's parents

   C. The amount of at-home reading the student engages in

   D. The frequency at which the student speaks the home language

10. Which of the following would be the most beneficial data teachers can use to determine if an ELL is having difficulty learning English because of a learning disability?

   A. Behavior records, culture shock, assimilation

   B. Metacognitive deficits, fluency data, writing samples

   C. Parent phone calls, observations, and writing samples

   D. Fluency data, homework assignments, cooperative learning

Assessment

Think Like a Test Maker

Number	Answer	Explanation
1.	D	The teacher is trying to diagnose the issue the student is having. Therefore, a diagnostic assessment is appropriate here.
2.	B	Above everything else, assessments should be used to make instructional decisions in the classroom.
3.	D	Formative assessments are often informal, ongoing checks that help a teacher decide how to move forward in a lesson. Remember formative assessments inform the instruction delivery.
4.	C	The anecdotes provide context and description of the student's interaction with text. As the teacher observes the student, the teacher can see what the student is doing and evaluate those behaviors.
5.	A	Extended time is the most common test accommodation for ELLs taking a state-standardized test. The test will always be in English, and students are required to answer questions in English. However, qualifying ELLs can receive extended time.
6.	B	Sequencing skills can be measured in an oral assessment by simply having the student tell, out loud, the story sequence. This is an example of an informal assessment accommodation.
7.	C	Students with special needs and learning disabilities will have an individual education plan (IEP). In the IEP are accommodations the teacher must follow for each student. Standards should be followed, and accommodations should be met.
8.	D	These students probably do not have learning disabilities; they are ELLs struggling with a new language. Therefore, the best answer is to use data from the diagnostic assessment to differentiate instruction and scaffold (support) instruction to accommodate these learners. Be on the lookout for answer choices that include an assumption that ELLs have learning disabilities. Avoid these answer choices. ELLs are disproportionately represented in special education programs when they do not have learning disabilities. You must know the difference between language learning and special needs.
9.	A	One of the biggest indicators of L2 success is the proficiency level of L1. If students are struggling in L1, they will also struggle in L2. Answer A is the most important consideration in this situation.
10.	B	Answer B is the only answer where cognitive ability is mentioned. That is the indicator teachers should use to determine if there is a learning disability.

Assessment

This page intentionally left blank.

VI – Advocating for ELLs – Knowledge of ESL/ESOL research, history, public policy, and current practices

Teachers and administrators must keep all stakeholders in mind when planning for the school. Stakeholders include parents from other cultures and backgrounds. Already mentioned in this book is the importance of making correspondence with parents comprehensible—sending information to parents in their home language. This practice of making education comprehensible for the student and parents is aligned to the Consent Decree.

The Consent Decree. Grounded in the 14th Amendment and the result of League of United Latin American Citizens (LULAC) vs. State Board of Education, the Consent Decree protects English Language Learners (ELL) and their right to a free, comprehensible education. It addresses civil and academic rights of ELLs and requires instruction be delivered in a comprehensible manner so ELLs can fully participate.

Major Court Cases and Policies Involving ELL Instruction

The following are state and federal laws addressing English as a Second Language (ESL) Education:

Title VI of the Civil Rights Act (1964) Title VI states, "No person in the United States shall, on the ground of race, or national origin, be excluded from participation in, be denied the benefits of, or otherwise be subjected to discrimination under any problem or activity receiving federal financial assistance from the Department of Health, Education, and Welfare" (Title VI of the CRS of 1964, US CFR Part 80).

Bilingual Education Act (1968) Congress legislated the Bilingual Education Act of 1968 in order to mandate schools to provide bilingual education programs. This was the first time Congress had endorsed funding for bilingual education. The Bilingual Program was a federally funded program through Title VII of the Elementary and Secondary Education Act, with the revision of Improving America's Schools Act of 1994.

Lau vs. Nichols, (494 U.S. Reports, 563-72 Oct. term, 1974) This is a landmark case pertaining to language minority education. The San Francisco school system failed to provide English language instruction to 1,800 limited-English proficient Chinese students. The Court of Appeals ruled that:

"Where inability to speak and understand the English language excludes national origin-minority group children from effective participation in the educational program offered by a school district, the district must take affirmative steps to rectify the language deficiency to open its instructional program to these students." 35 Fed. Reg. 11595.

"Students must receive instruction from properly certified, licensed teachers." (511 IAC 6.1-3- 1.d)

"Each school corporation shall provide appropriate instruction to limited English proficient students." (511 IAC 6.1-5-8)

Equal Education Opportunities Act (1974) This act insures equal education rights for language minority students.

Castaneda v. Picard (648 F.2n.989, 1981) The Court of Appeals articulated a three-part test for assessing a school system's treatment of limited English proficient students. The standard requires (1) a sound approach to the education of these students, (2) reasonable implementation of the approach, and (3) outcomes reflecting that the approach is working.

Plyer vs. Doe (102 S. Ct. 2382, 1982) The United States Supreme Court stated that school systems must enroll and educate children residing in their district even if their parents do not possess legal residency documents.

Every Student Succeeds Act (ESSA) Signed by President Obama in 2015, ESSA includes important policies that recognize the needs and diversity of English learners (ELs) to close the achievement gap between them and other students. The bill, which reauthorizes the Elementary and Secondary Education Act, also crucially maintains accountability for how ELLs are educated, known as the No Child Left Behind Act.

No Child Left Behind (NCLB) The main law for K–12 general education in the United States from 2002–2015 was NCLB. The law focused on standards-based instruction and held schools and teachers accountable for student test scores.

Family Educational Rights and Privacy Act (FERPA) FERPA is a Federal law that protects the privacy of student education records. The law applies to all schools that receive funds under an applicable program of the U.S. Department of Education.

FERPA gives parents certain rights with respect to their children's education records. These rights transfer to the student when he or she reaches the age of 18 or attends a school beyond the high school level (U.S. Department of Education, 2019).

Individuals with Disabilities Education Act (IDEA) is a law that makes available a free appropriate public education to eligible children with disabilities throughout the nation and ensures special education and related services to those children.

Section 504 of the Rehabilitation Act of 1973 Section 504 regulations require a school district to provide a free appropriate public education (FAPE) to each qualified student with a disability who is in the school district's jurisdiction, regardless of the nature or severity of the disability. Under Section 504, FAPE consists of the provision of regular or special education and related aids and services designed to meet the student's individual educational needs as adequately as the needs of nondisabled students are met (U.S. Department of Education, 2015).

Think Like a Test Maker

Not all laws have been enacted to protect ELLs. Many lawmakers have proposed limiting bilingual education in favor of English only practices. Proposition 227 in California, Proposition 203 in Arizona, and Question 2 in Massachusetts all resulted in major restrictions in bilingual education and enforced English only practices.

Appropriate strategies that help ELLs

Total Physical Response (TPR) uses movement to teach language and vocabulary. It mimics the way infants use language. Examples include:

- Head, shoulders, knees, and toes
- The teacher models and students perform the action
- Simon Says

Cognitive Academic Language Learning Approach (CALLA) consists of metacognitive, cognitive, and social strategies

Sheltered Instruction Observation Protocol (SIOP) is a research-based instructional model that is effective in developing the academic skills of ELLs. The SIOP consists of eight components:

1. Lesson Preparation
2. Building Background
3. Comprehensible Input
4. Strategies
5. Interaction
6. Practice/Application
7. Lesson Delivery
8. Review & Assessment

Disabilities vs Language Barriers

It is important that teachers distinguish between language difficulty and learning disabilities. Often, ELLs are overrepresented in special education programs. The overrepresentation of ELLs in special education classes is one of the critical issues affecting this group of students. Research indicates that one of the factors affecting this overrepresentation of ELLs is the difficulty educators have in distinguishing students who truly have special education needs from students who are learning English as a second language (Artiles & Klingner, 2006). ELLs are disadvantaged by the lack of appropriate assessments and personnel trained to conduct culturally valid educational assessments.

However, some ELLs do have learning disabilities and special needs and do qualify for special services. ELLs who need special education services need educators trained to address students' language and disability needs simultaneously.

Providing special education students access to the general curriculum is mandated under The Individuals with Disabilities Education Act (IDEA). Instructional supports, inclusive classroom practices, parent involvement, appropriate accommodations and modifications, updated IEPs, are all examples of helping these students access general education curriculum. This is often referred to as the least restrictive environment (LRE).

For the exam, make sure you know common strategies for helping special education students access the general education curriculum:

- Help students with their social skills because social skills are necessary for general education and cooperative learning.

- Differentiate instruction because that addresses students' learning profiles, which includes learning styles, environmental factors that affect the students' learning, and students' grouping preferences.

- Read students' IEPs and plan instruction according to their needed accommodations and their academic and behavioral goals.

- Keep standards high while also providing accommodations and modifications to help students access and meet those standards.

- Use common modifications to activities and assignments to help students achieve their goals. These include giving students extra time, using small groups for assignments, allowing students to use audio components or large print, and using sensory tools.

When the needs of a special education student are not met in the general education classes, supplementary or functional curriculum may be necessary. Implementing supplementary or functional aids should be used to keep students in LRE and educated as much as possible with their peers who are not in special education.

Advocating for ELLs

Remember, the goal is inclusion, so supplementary and functional curriculum is there to keep students in the general classroom as much as possible.

Legal provisions provide a framework for providing ELLs with disabilities with appropriate services for both their English language acquisition and specific disability.

The following are effective practices in the ESOL classroom

- Prevention and early intervention services to avoid unnecessary special education referrals. Use MTSS as much as possible. See the Cultural Awareness section of the book for more on MTSS.

- Use referral processes that differentiate struggling learners from those who have learning disabilities or special needs.

- Assessments should be conducted by qualified bilingual evaluators who use culturally valid instruments appropriate for ELLs. These instruments must provide accurate data about native language and English language performance (L1 and L2).

Think Like a Test Maker

Be on the lookout for questions about the home language survey (HLS). This is a questionnaire given to parents or guardians as soon as their student enrolls in school. This survey helps schools identify which students are ELL and whether they are eligible for language assistance services.

- Use of interpreters for non-English speaking parents.

- Individualized Education Programs (IEPs) that are culturally and linguistically relevant and that describe how services for English language acquisition and academic instruction should be provided simultaneously.

- Incorporate diversity in the classroom.

- Celebrate cultural differences.

- Serve as an advocate for ELL and special education students.

- Pay attention to preferred learning styles (multiple intelligences).

- Know factors that contribute to cultural bias (e.g., stereotyping, prejudice, ethnocentrism) and how to create a culturally responsive learning environment.

Gifted ELLs

Conventional methods for identifying students who are gifted are usually based on assessment data and previous high academic achievement. This can be inequitable for ELLs whose language output and cultural orientation may mask their giftedness. Therefore, it is important to use other methods for identifying students who are ELL and gifted.

A more inclusive framework includes several components, such as a comprehensive definition of exceptional ability that encompasses more than just scores and includes cognitive, social, emotional, artistic, linguistic, and logical-reasoning competencies. A more inclusive framework would also include multiple entry points beyond the standard gifted assessments. These qualitative measures would include student interviews, performance-based evaluations, or nonverbal instruments and can be effective in identifying gifted students. Teachers should also be on the lookout for alternative ways ELLs show that they are gifted.

ELLs who may be gifted:

- Acquire the new language faster than other ELLs

- Code switch or translate at an advanced level

- Show ability in converting between cultures

- Display leadership and/or imaginative qualities

- Read above grade level in the first language

- Exhibit rapid integration into American culture

- Problem-solve in creative ways

Quick Tip

Current screening protocols are not designed to detect ELLs who are gifted. Widening the net to move beyond isolated quantitative data points (this is true for all students not just ELLs) and toward qualitative portfolios will help to identify and serve marginalized populations typically not identified as gifted.

Motivation

Intrinsic motivation

Intrinsic motivation is behavior driven by internal rewards rather than external rewards. According to self-determination theory, intrinsic motivation is driven by three things: autonomy, relatedness, and competence.

- **Autonomy**. This has to do with students' independence and self-governance. Allowing students to decide how and what they learn helps to increase autonomy and motivation. Students should be permitted to self-select books and work on things that interest them.

- **Relatedness.** Students must see the value in what they are learning as it pertains to their everyday lives. The best teachers make learning relatable and applicable to the real world.

- **Competence.** Students must feel they are equipped to meet your expectations. It is important to challenge students while also providing them with activities based on readiness levels and ability.

Extrinsic motivation

Extrinsic motivation refers to behavior that is driven by external rewards. Providing students with a party if they reach their reading goal or allowing students extra playtime because they cleaned up the classroom are examples of extrinsic motivation. Grades can also be considered extrinsic rewards. Extrinsic motivation is often unsustainable because once the reward is removed, the student is no longer motivated to achieve.

Think Like a Test Maker

Integrative motivation is a type of motivation that refers to a learner's intrinsic orientation or desire to communicate with, be more like, or to join the L2 (second or foreign language) user community.

Advocating for ELLs

This page intentionally left blank.

1. Which of the following practices are most effective when planning for student-led conferences with parents whose first language is not English?

    A. Deliver information in a comprehensible manner.

    B. Allow the student to translate for the parents.

    C. Request that a co-teacher translate during the conferences.

    D. Require the student to speak English only during the conference.

2. A teacher wants to increase students' integrative motivation. Which of the following activities would achieve that?

    A. Have students take regular standardized tests.

    B. Have students engage in role play.

    C. Regularly call home to tell parents students' accomplishments.

    D. Provide specific and meaningful feedback.

3. Which TWO of the following would be considered extrinsic motivators?

    A. Desire to do well

    B. Extra credit

    C. Praise

    D. Autonomy

4. An ELL student is also in a special needs class. What would be the most appropriate placement for the student during a science lab?

    A. In the back of the room

    B. In the front of the room

    C. In the least restrictive environment

    D. With a paraprofessional

5. Juan is an ELL who struggles with the content and may be displaying cognitive impairments. However, the teacher is unsure. What should the teacher do in this situation?

    A. Refer Juan to the special education program.

    B. Call Juan's parents and discuss options.

    C. Have a qualified bilingual evaluator assess Juan's skills.

    D. Request a special education and ESOL paraprofessional for Juan.

6. Which of the following can be used before testing an ELL for special education and as interventions to mitigate the need for an IEP?

   A. Multi-tiered system of supports

   B. Behavioral management

   C. Regular testing in the home language

   D. Parent-teacher conferences

7. Which of the following ensures that students, regardless of citizenship, receive a free, comprehensible, public education?

   A. Civil Rights Act of 1968

   B. Castaneda v. Picard

   C. Every Student Succeeds Act (ESSA)

   D. The Consent Decree

8. Which of the following has to do with students' right to self-governance and motivation to learn?

   A. Autonomy

   B. Relatedness

   C. Self-advocacy

   D. Competence

9. Which of the following is a learning approach that is focused on social activities for ELLs?

   A. BICS

   B. CALPS

   C. CALLA

   D. TPR

10. Which of the following is the best way for teachers to advocate for their ELL students?

    A. Allow students to work with their peers as much as possible, so they feel comfortable sharing in the learning.

    B. Provide a comprehensible education that is aligned to the standards and scaffold when students need support.

    C. Regularly test students and place them in the appropriate groups so they receive their proper accommodations.

    D. Include parents in the planning process of the ELLs academic plans and continually check in with parents regarding goals.

Number	Answer	Explanation
1.	A	The word comprehensible is a good word for this section of the exam. It has to do with making sure parents and students understand what is being communicated. A teacher would let the student translate for the parents, as in answer B. However, delivering information in a comprehensible manner is most effective. Answers C and D are not at all effective and should be avoided.
2.	B	Integrative motivation is a type of motivation that refers to a learner's intrinsic orientation or desire to communicate with, be more like, or join the L2 (second or foreign language) user community. Therefore, roleplay is the best activity for this situation.
3.	B & C	Extra credit and praise are both extrinsic motivators because the motivation is external.
4.	C	Students with disabilities should always be placed in the least restrictive environment. That means they should be with their peers participating as long as they are safe to do so.
5.	C	To be sure Juan is being evaluated properly, having a skilled evaluator in both special needs and language acquisition is key. Juan is displaying cognitive impairments, which may be a sign of learning disabilities. However, a skilled bilingual evaluator will be able to determine if it is a language issue or a cognitive issue.
6.	A	The MTSS framework is evidence-based and has had a significant impact on addressing the needs of different subgroups of students. MTSS can be an effective approach for ELLs who struggle.
7.	D	Consent Decree protects English language learners (ELLs) and their right to a free, comprehensible education. It addresses civil and academic rights of ELLs and requires that instruction be delivered in a comprehensible manner so ELLs can fully participate.
8.	A	Autonomy has to do with students' independence and self-governance. Allowing students to decide how and what they learn helps to increase autonomy and increase motivation. Students should be permitted to self-select books and work on things that interest them.
9.	A	BICS Stands for basic interpersonal communication skills and is the best choice for this scenario. The other answer choices focus on academic language acquisition.
10.	B	Answer B has all the best practices and phrases—comprehensible, standards aligned, scaffolding.

This page intentionally left blank.

1. Which of the following teaching strategies would best show sensitivity to ELLs' language challenges?

    A. Displaying the students' uncorrected English work in the classroom.

    B. Grouping students by their English knowledge and experience.

    C. Using ancillary materials aligned to the standards to support comprehensible delivery of instruction.

    D. Assigning students whose first language is English to tutor classmates.

2. An ELL is struggling in science class. The text is complex, and the student has limited English proficiency. What would be the most effective approach for a teacher to make to help this student?

    A. Focus only on what the student can read so the student can understand the concepts.

    B. Continue teaching grade-level science text while using scaffolding and supports for the ELL.

    C. Have the student work with a buddy on reading techniques for science.

    D. Let the parents know that at-home practice is necessary for the student to succeed.

3. Which of the following would be most effective when assisting ELLs in literacy and academic language development?

    A. Apply real-world concepts to content area text.

    B. Use a system of rewards for reaching literacy goals.

    C. Focus on vocabulary acquisition.

    D. Focus on roleplay and social learning.

4. Which of the following activities would be most appropriate in teaching students persuasive writing?

    A. Make a brochure about the cell.

    B. Write a letter to parents about their day at school.

    C. Build a website with text explaining pictures on the site.

    D. Write an email to the principal about allowing cultural celebrations.

5. A teacher has several ELLs in class and knows they will struggle with the academic language specific to a science unit. Which of the following activities would be most effective to help support students before reading the science unit?

    A. Show a short video clip where many of the complex concepts and vocab are addressed.

    B. Have students write down the difficult vocabulary and write definitions.

    C. Allow the students to skip over difficult vocabulary in the reading section.

    D. Pair the ELLs with other students who can translate the information.

6. Which of the following is most effective when teaching students speaking and listening skills in academic and social situations?

    A. Students watch videos on appropriate communication.

    B. The teacher has parents work with students at home on communication.

    C. The teacher models appropriate and effective communication.

    D. Students read about effective communication.

7. What is most beneficial regarding flexible grouping when working with ELLs on second language acquisition?

    A. Flexible grouping allows the teacher to differentiate in real time.

    B. Flexible grouping lets students work with new people all the time.

    C. Flexible grouping switches things up so the students don't get bored.

    D. Flexible grouping allows the teacher time to transition to new activities.

8. Which of the following supports reading and writing English?

    A. Have students write new English vocabulary words and their definitions.

    B. Align instruction and activities to English language arts standards

    C. Have students work in cooperative groups to help each other learn.

    D. Work with a paraprofessional to ensure translation services.

9. Which of the following activities would best measure mastery of a particular concept?

    A. A multiple-choice test

    B. A flexible grouping activity

    C. A read-aloud activity

    D. A critical thinking activity

10. Which of the following would be most effective when teaching ELLs in a science class?

    A. Focus on science vocabulary and have students write and memorize.

    B. Use word analysis to show students the importance of phonics in learning a new language.

    C. Integrate listening, speaking, reading, and writing at varying English proficiency levels.

    D. Use roleplay and vocabulary instruction when needed.

11. A teacher is putting groups of students together with mixed abilities and reading levels. This is called:

    A. Interest grouping

    B. Homogeneous grouping

    C. Heterogeneous grouping

    D. Peer-tutoring grouping

12. A teacher notices a few students are not motivated to read the current section of a piece of informational text. What can the teacher do to motivate students to engage in the reading?

    A. Allow the students to self-select books from a standards-aligned group of informational texts.

    B. Allow students to partner up and read the text with a buddy.

    C. Reward the students with extra time in the computer lab for finishing the reading.

    D. Require the students to finish the reading for homework.

13. A teacher has several ELL students who are not yet fluent in English. The teacher also has students who are struggling in fluency. Which of the following activities would help these students with fluency, confidence, and reading aloud?

    A. Silent sustained reading

    B. Popcorn reading

    C. Round robin reading

    D. Choral reading

14. A social science teacher is working on a lesson about WWII. The teacher knows students will struggle with the informational text. What can a teacher use to help intermediate ELLs grapple with the text while also organizing their learning?

    A. Have students work in cooperative groups

    B. Have students use a graphic organizer

    C. Have paraprofessional assist students with translation

    D. Have students read more about WWII at home.

15. A teacher wants to use literature circles in her class. What is the most appropriate structure for organization and instruction?

    A. Whole group to model how to read text aloud

    B. Small group differentiated cooperative learning

    C. Direct instruction to address the entire class

    D. Individual conferencing to set goals

16. Ms. Ruiz is an introductory writing teacher with a diverse class consisting of students from a variety of cultural and linguistic backgrounds. During a writing assignment, she has students brainstorm ideas. What would be the best way to encourage these students in this activity?

    A. Encourage ELLs to use their cultural backgrounds and language to brainstorm ideas.

    B. Encourage ELLs to use the textbook to guide brainstorming ideas.

    C. Have students rely on their paraprofessionals for brainstorming ideas.

    D. Have students consult English dictionaries before brainstorming ideas.

17. Which of the following activities would be most appropriate for ELLs who learn kinesthetically?

    A. An essay assignment

    B. A cooperative learning assignment

    C. A physical activity

    D. A reading activity

18. A teacher is allowing ELLs to choose how they will show mastery of a particular concept. The teacher is allowing students to choose from the following to produce as a measure of standards mastery: a brochure, a podcast, a game, a presentation. What is the teacher considering when she allows students to choose how they show mastery?

    A. Learning preferences

    B. Assessment outcomes

    C. Collaboration

    D. State tests

19. A teacher has a few students who need specific reading interventions. What would be the most effective way to organize these interventions in the classroom?

    A. Have the paraprofessional work with students who need help and focus instruction to students who have met proficiency.

    B. Use a whole group approach to address the reading deficiencies and apply strategies when needed.

    C. Set up a variety of reading centers that target reading interventions, use flexible grouping to move students through the centers, and monitor progress by observing students.

    D. Group all struggling readers together, apply interventions, and allow grade-level readers to engage in an activity of their choice.

20. A student scores consistently in the top percentile of the class on tests and quizzes. However, the student rarely interacts with the reading assignments. What can the teacher do to help motivate this student to put effort toward reading time?

    A. Allow the student time to go to the library provided he finishes his classwork and homework.

    B. Send detailed weekly reports home to his parents so they can encourage him to finish homework.

    C. Document how many times he finishes his homework and reward him when he reaches three days in a row.

    D. Conference with the student and determine activities that will challenge the student while also allowing him to show mastery of the standards.

21. When a student has awareness of phonemes in words, syllables, onset-rime segments, and spelling, he or she is demonstrating:

    A. Phonological awareness

    B. Phonics mastery

    C. Phonemic awareness

    D. Structural analysis

Think Like a Test Maker

22. Phonemic awareness includes the ability to:

    A. Form compound words and combine word parts

    B. Spell accurately and decode unfamiliar words

    C. Pronounce individual sounds in words

    D. Differentiate between homonyms and spell accurately

23. A teacher is working with a student on initial sounds. The teacher says *pet* and asks the student to replace the initial consonant to make other words, such as *get*, *vet*, and *set*. What is this an example of?

    A. Segmenting

    B. Blending

    C. Structural analysis

    D. Substituting

24. A reading teacher wants to help students with segmentation. What is the most appropriate instructional approach?

    A. Have students break apart words by separate phonemes.

    B. Have students break apart compound words.

    C. Have students blend beginning consonants together.

    D. Have students use prefixes and suffixes to learn words.

25. Which word is correctly broken up by onset and rime?

    A. /mon/ -/key/

    B. /t/- /ap/

    C. /hand/- /y/

    D. /pro/-/tect/

26. A student in the partial-alphabetic phase says the word *sun* and identifies the /s/ and /n/ sounds. What would be the most appropriate next step to take with this student?

    A. Identify all three letters in the word.

    B. Identify medial sounds in words.

    C. Decode the word by using grammar rules.

    D. String together blends in words.

27. A teacher has posted words next to everyday objects in the classroom—door, pencils, library, sink. The teacher is developing students':

    A. Phonemic awareness

    B. Morphology

    C. Spelling

    D. Environmental print

28. A student draws a stick figure and scribbles above the picture. The student says, "This says, 'Sarah is my best friend.'" What can the teacher determine from this behavior?

   A. The student needs assistance with fine motor skills.

   B. The student is ready for phonics instruction using single syllable words.

   C. The student understands directionality of print.

   D. The student can distinguish between pictures and print.

29. Which of the following would be most appropriate for a kindergarten class learning the alphabetic principle?

   A. When students speak, write on the board snippets of what they say.

   B. Have students read aloud in class to a partner.

   C. Administer regular spelling tests.

   D. Have students write down words they do not understand.

30. Why is teaching phonological generalizations better than teaching phonological rules?

   A. Students don't need to follow all the phonological rules.

   B. Words always follow phonological rules.

   C. Words never follow phonological rules.

   D. Some words don't follow phonological rules.

31. When students look at other words, pictures, and graphics to figure out words, they are using:

   A. Prefixes and suffixes

   B. Word analysis

   C. Morphological analysis

   D. Semantic cueing

32. Which of the following sets of letters would a teacher use when helping students with their diphthongs?

   A. *oi, ai, ei*

   B. *kn, gn, gh*

   C. *ee, ea, oo*

   D. *ff, ll, pp*

33. Which of the following would be most appropriate to strengthen automatic word recognition skills?

   A. Memorize high frequency words.

   B. Have students track letters with a finger as they read.

   C. Write down difficult words over and over.

   D. Use a dictionary for unfamiliar words.

34. Which of the following represents an error in decoding vowel teams?

    A. During a spelling test, the student writes *cone* when the teacher sad *coin*.

    B. During a fluency read, the student reads *cone* when the word is *coin*.

    C. During a spelling test, the student writes *bake* when the teacher sad *back*.

    D. During a fluency read, the student reads *bake* when the word is *back*.

35. Which of the following students would benefit most from explicit phonics instruction?

    A. A pre-school student who knows the alphabet but cannot recognize phonemes in words.

    B. A kindergarten student who can recognize pictures and associate them with words.

    C. A first-grade student who has memorized 100 sight words but cannot decode medium-frequency words in text.

    D. A third-grade student who has automaticity but struggles with low-frequency, academic words in text.

36. A teacher is determining if students are ready to move on to phonics instruction. Which of the following skills on the phonological awareness continuum should she be looking for before starting explicit phonics instruction?

    A. Students can identify the number of sounds in a word.

    B. Students can segment words and blend sounds in words.

    C. Students can isolate the sounds in words.

    D. Student can clap two-syllable words.

37. Which of the following is the order in which students acquire skills?

    A. Comprehension, fluency, decoding

    B. Fluency, decoding, comprehension

    C. Decoding, comprehension, fluency

    D. Decoding, fluency, comprehension

38. Which of the following is a CVCe word?

    A. Crank

    B. Mat

    C. Mate

    D. Believe

39. A teacher is explaining that some words occur frequently in text, and some do not follow the rules of phonics. Which instructional approach would be most effective here?

    A. Use word analysis.

    B. Use phonemic awareness.

    C. Use sight word memorization.

    D. Use decoding strategies.

40. Use the table to match the activity with the skill.

Skill
Compound sentences
Modal verbs
Topic sentence and supporting details
Speaking and listening

Activity
Roleplay
Using conjunctions to join clauses
Placing words like *should*, *could*, and *must* properly in a sentence
Organizing sentences in a logical order

41. Which of the following would be most appropriate to use to teach basic English syntax to third-grade ELLs?

    A. Identifying the subject and predicate of a sentence.

    B. Writing an essay with proper grammar and punctuation.

    C. Identifying digraphs in words.

    D. Breaking apart compound words.

42. Which of the following best displays the proper stress for the word *information*?

    A. ●●⬤●

    B. ●⬤●●

    C. ●●●⬤

    D. ⬤●●●

43. This is the idea that there are two independent ways in which students develop their linguistic skills.

    A. Acquisition-learning hypothesis

    B. Monitor hypothesis

    C. Input hypothesis

    D. Affective filter hypothesis

    E. Natural order hypothesis

44. A student is speaking with a teacher about the sequence of a story. The student corrects herself when she makes mistakes. This aligns with:

    A. Acquisition-learning hypothesis

    B. Monitor hypothesis

    C. Input hypothesis

    D. Affective filter hypothesis

    E. Natural order hypothesis

Think Like a Test Maker

45. A student is speaking to the teacher and asks, "What is that tool, like a spoon but cuts? How do you say?" This is an example of:

   A. Overgeneralization

   B. Circumlocution

   C. Simplification

   D. Affect filter

46. Students are in the beginning stages of second language acquisition and are using the past tense *ed* after verbs, even irregular verbs. For example, students say **sleeped** instead of **slept** and **rided** instead of **rode**. The students are using:

   A. Circumlocution

   B. Simplification

   C. Affect filter

   D. Overgeneralization

47. Which of the following practices is most effective for both ELLs and native English speakers in developing mastery in two languages?

   A. Isolation

   B. Simplification

   C. Dual immersion

   D. Early exit

48. What is the most effective way to engage students who are working on second language acquisition?

   A. Convey high expectations and align instruction to the standards.

   B. Focus on cooperative learning so students can interact.

   C. Ask for a paraprofessional to come in three times a week to translate instruction.

   D. Use dictionaries to translate L1 to L2.

49. Which of the following factors should be considered when teaching ELLs?

   A. Bilingual education is essential because it considers the role of culture in language and helps students develop advanced cognitive skills.

   B. Focusing on English only will help students learn the second language more quickly than if both languages are used.

   C. Group work should be the main method of curriculum because it includes social interaction and conversation.

   D. Teachers should delay learning in the second language until students master their first language.

50. A teacher is having students role-play a scenario at a grocery store. Students are using conversation in a real-world setting to strengthen their L2 skills. What type of activity is this?

    A. Monitor

    B. CALP

    C. BICS

    D. Natural Order

51. Second language acquisition is a nonlinear process marked by rapid progression in some areas and stagnation in others because of the influence of the first language. This is called:

    A. Pragmatics

    B. Interlanguage

    C. Semantics

    D. Transfer

52. Two students from Cambodia attend content area classes in a classroom separate from the mainstream classes so they can focus on academic achievement while working on their language skills. This type of instruction is called:

    A. Immersion

    B. Bilingual

    C. Cooperative

    D. Sheltered

53. An ELL who achieves more through using manipulatives and hands-on activities than she does reading aloud has what type of learning preference?

    A. Kinesthetic

    B. Visual

    C. Auditory

    D. Spatial

54. An eighth-grade ELL has just exited the ESOL program and will be entering a regular English class. What would be the most effective way for the general education English teacher to support the student who will be reading complex literary novels in class?

    A. Find the same novels adapted to a lower grade level for the student to read.

    B. Have the student work primarily with another ESL student so they can translate for each other.

    C. Work with the student before and after school, so the student can acquire the advance skills needed.

    D. Chunk sections of the novels so the student can read pieces of the text at a time and derive meaning.

55. A ninth-grade teacher is helping ELLs read aloud in small groups. One student stumbles over several words, becomes very frustrated, and shuts down. What can the teacher do to help this student feel more comfortable and motivated to continue with the reading?

    A. Lower the affective filter

    B. Increase the affective filter

    C. Reward the student

    D. Allow the student to take a break

56. A student is reading but having trouble understanding a common idiom in an English text. The teacher tries to explain but the student is confused. Which would be the best way to help the student understand the idiomatic language?

    A. Have the student translate the idiom into his first language.

    B. Have the student look up the words of the idiom in a dictionary.

    C. Use visual representations to support understanding of the idiomatic language.

    D. Have the student skip over the idiom and continue reading.

57. An ESL teacher understands that her ELLs will have a difficult time understanding a piece of complex text. What can the teacher do to prepare students for this task?

    A. Activate their background knowledge by discussing the vocabulary and major concepts of the reading before the reading starts.

    B. Assign homework the night before for students to do so they are prepared for the reading the next day.

    C. Have students work in pairs to partner read so they do not feel overwhelmed by the reading.

    D. Write out notes in English for the ELLs so they can reference them during the reading.

58. A student is in the early stages of language acquisition. Which of the following activities would be most beneficial to this student when learning science concepts about the life cycle of the frog?

    A. Write down the vocab and their definitions they student will see in the science text.

    B. Have another student translate the main concepts for the ELL.

    C. Have students draw pictures of the life cycle of the frog.

    D. Ask for the paraprofessional to work 1-1 with the student to explain the concept.

59. An ELL is reading to the teacher in a 1-1 session. As the student reads, he stumbles over a few words but quickly corrects himself. Which of the following is the student engaging in?

    A. Input

    B. Output

    C. Monitor

    D. Natural order

Practice Test 1

60. Which of the following would be most effective for a student in the beginning stages of language acquisition to strengthen oral skills?

A. Have the student write down the beginning, middle, and end of a story.

B. Have the student complete at-home practice in reading.

C. Have the student summarize a story in his home language then translate it to English.

D. Have a student narrate a wordless picture book and explain the main parts of the story.

61. Two-way immersion program is beneficial because it promotes:

A. Assimilation

B. Acculturation

C. Sheltered instruction

D. Additive bilingualism

62. A new teacher is working on professional development that will help the teacher to be culturally responsive to ELLs. Which of the following areas would be most beneficial to this teacher in this area?

A. Semantics

B. Sociolinguistics

C. Phonemic awareness

D. Emersion

63. When the teacher engages with an ELL's parents in a conference, through a translator, the parents say that the student will not speak their home language anymore and has stopped participating in some family traditions. Explain the likely situation happening with this student.

A. The student is trying to assimilate to the new culture so the student can fit in.

B. The student is using acculturation by merging old traditions with new.

C. The student is changing dialect so they can communicate with peers.

D. The student does not understand register and is failing to communicate properly.

64. A social studies teacher recently welcomed a new ELL to the class. Which of the following would be most appropriate for this student?

A. Have the student introduce himself to the class and talk about where he is from.

B. Meet with the student's parents as soon as possible to determine what the student needs.

C. Meet with the student privately to welcome him to the class and review routines.

D. Group the student with other ELLs so they can translate for each other when needed.

Think Like a Test Maker

65. A teacher wants students to engage in a prereading strategy to activate background knowledge. She hopes the session will help the student understand the text. Which of the following would be most effective for this exercise?

   A. Provide students with an English dictionary so they can translate their brainstorming sessions.

   B. Provide students with an outline in English that details the text main subjects so the students can use it during brainstorming.

   C. Require students to use English only so they can immerse themselves in the new language for more success in reading.

   D. Encourage students to brainstorm in their home language and draw from experiences in their cultures.

66. Maria has been in the U.S. for several years. She lives in a Puerto Rican community and speaks Spanish in the home. She is fluent in English but still makes small grammatical errors in her written and verbal communication. This does not impede her ability to achieve in school or communicate. Which of the following is most likely contributing to these small errors she makes when communicating in English?

   A. Assimilation

   B. Acculturation

   C. Fossilization

   D. Equilibrium

67. A teacher notices that a student stutters in class when she is using L2. The student is in the beginning stages of language acquisition. However, the teacher also notices when the student is speaking with friends in the lunchroom, she does not stutter. What should the teacher do?

   A. Request the student receive an evaluation for special education services.

   B. Investigate further and see if the student stutters in her L1.

   C. Ask that a speech pathologist be assigned to the student during reading class.

   D. Have the student read aloud more frequently so she can practice getting better.

68. A teacher is using roleplay and communication to support students' learning of L2. Which of the following approaches is the teacher employing?

   A. Social interactionist

   B. Whole language

   C. Stages of language acquisition

   D. Phonological Awareness

69. Which of the following is most culturally responsive for a fifth-grade classroom and will help develop self-esteem and pride around students' cultures and differences?

   A. Have students show their cultural traditions and backgrounds to the class in a presentation.

   B. Have students work in small groups to discuss their cultural backgrounds, food, and traditions. Encourage them to ask questions.

   C. Have students interview their parents about their traditions and cultural celebrations and write an essay explaining them.

   D. Celebrate a different culture each week by reading about the culture in class.

70. Which of the following aligns to what social linguists study?

   A. Grammar

   B. Spelling

   C. Pragmatics

   D. Semantics

71. Why is it important for ESL/ESOL teachers to include cultures and traditions in reading and writing lessons?

   A. Language and culture are interrelated

   B. This will lower the affective filter

   C. This will increase the affective filter

   D. Students feel more comfortable

72. A group of ELLs who are at the intermediate level of language acquisition but hesitant to respond to questions and rarely speak during class discussions may be:

   A. Going through acculturation

   B. Reverting to the silent period

   C. Used to a student-centered classroom

   D. Used to a teacher-centered classroom

73. What can a teacher do to ensure her ELL students feel safe and empowered to engage in classroom activities?

   A. Relate the nature and role of culture, cultural groups, and individual cultural identities into learning experiences for all students.

   B. Require students who are ELL to partner with other students who are ELL so everyone feels comfortable in the classroom setting.

   C. Attend professional development on multicultural teaching in a diverse classroom.

   D. Ask a peer mentor to observe how she is teaching and if it is aligned to multicultural guidelines.

74. Mr. Taft is assessing students' comprehension of text by giving them an assignment on story sequence. What is the best way to accommodate a student in this situation who has oral fluency but not written fluency?

   A. Allow the student to demonstrate mastery by telling the sequence of events in the story.

   B. Require the student to write the sequence of events in the story.

   C. Allow the student to use a Spanish to English dictionary.

   D. Have the paraprofessional write the sequence of events in the story as the student dictates them.

75. Which of the following should a teacher consider first when planning a lesson for students who are ELL?

   A. The students' stages of language acquisition

   B. The students' interest in the material being presented

   C. The district policy on teaching ELL students

   D. The state adopted academic standards

76. Piyush is a student from India who has formal English language training and who does very well on L2 reading and writing. He is highly motivated to increase his conversational English so he can converse with his peers. What type of motivation is this?

    A. Extrinsic

    B. Implicit

    C. Integrative

    D. Behavioral

77. A 10th grade biology teacher wants to help students with their cognitive academic language (CALP) by helping to minimize context-reduced situations in class. What can the teacher do to achieve this goal?

    A. Use mainly biology lectures to convey concepts to students.

    B. Have students complete research papers on different biology concepts.

    C. Have students work in groups and discuss biology concepts.

    D. Assess students regularly on biology concepts.

78. Which of the following would be a motivating factor for ELLs to work on their English skills?

    A. To do better in school and earn good grades

    B. To be able to communicate with peers

    C. To assimilate into the dominant culture

    D. To replace L1 with L2

79. In a fifth-grade class, the teacher uses her pointer finger to signal to an ELL to "come here." As students are playing on the playground, the ELL comes over but is visibly upset. The student cannot explain why. What might the teacher do to mitigate this situation in the future?

    A. Research hand gestures and their meaning in other cultures.

    B. Take the student to an interpreter and figure out why she is so upset.

    C. Allow the student to sit out for a while until she calms down.

    D. Refrain from using any hand signals because every student responds differently to them.

80. Which of the following describes a student-centered classroom that is culturally responsive?

    A. Setting clear goals for students, monitoring those goals, and celebrating success in second language acquisition.

    B. Allowing for frequent cooperative learning, discussion and debates on current events, metacognitive strategies.

    C. Using visual elements to supplement text, explicit whole-group instruction, student-led conferences with parents.

    D. Providing a safe space for student to take risks in learning, celebrating success, allowing for multiple ways to show mastery of high standards.

81. How do criterion-referenced assessments differ from norm-referenced assessments?

    A. Criterion-referenced assessments measure the average score while the norm-referenced assessments are based on a curve.

    B. Norm-referenced assessments measures student performance against a fixed set of predetermined criteria, and criterion-referenced assessments are designed to compare and rank test takers in relation to one another.

    C. Criterion-referenced measures student performance against a fixed set of predetermined criteria, and norm-referenced assessments are designed to compare and rank test takers in relation to one another.

    D. A criterion-referenced assessment happens throughout learning while a norm-referenced assessment happens at the end of learning.

82. When data from a language proficiency test can be applied to the real-world, the test has:

    A. Internal validity

    B. External validity

    C. Accuracy

    D. Reliability

83. The quality of getting consistent results on an assessment is known as:

    A. Internal validity

    B. External validity

    C. Formative assessment

    D. Reliability

84. Assessments used to measure standards mastery and expertise are:

    A. Labs, notebooks, running records, homework assignments

    B. Norm-referenced tests, homework assignments, quizzes

    C. Observations, checklists, surveys

    D. Research papers, presentations, formal debates

85. What can a teacher do to ensure that the tests are providing her with accurate measures of her students' abilities?

    A. Use a variety of formal and informal assessments.

    B. Use tests that are in the back of the textbook.

    C. Only use state standardized tests.

    D. Only use formative assessments.

86. Which of the following is most appropriate to use when setting expectations for a writing assignment?

    A. Portfolio

    B. Rubric

    C. Criterion assessment

    D. Norm-referenced assessment

Think Like a Test Maker

87. A teacher is trying to identify which skill an ELL is missing during reading instruction. What type of assessment would be most effective in this situation?

    A. Norm-referenced

    B. Criterion

    C. Diagnostic

    D. Portfolio

88. A science teacher plans to administer a chapter test that includes multiple choice and short answer. Which of the following accommodations is most appropriate for intermediate ELLs?

    A. Permitting the ELLs to use their textbooks during the test.

    B. Allowing the ELLs to take the test in their home language.

    C. Providing the ELLs with extra time to finish the short answer section.

    D. Having a paraprofessional translate the test to the ELLs.

89. An ESOL teacher plans to show parents student progress during student-led conferences at the end of the semester. Which type of assessment would be most beneficial to use?

    A. Norm-referenced

    B. Observation

    C. Multiple-choice

    D. Portfolio

90. Which of the following is the most effective way to use formative assessments?

    A. To rank students

    B. To monitor progress

    C. To measure outcomes

    D. To grade on a curve

91. A 7th grade teacher is going over parts of a cell with students. For the assessment, students must perform an identification activity where they label parts of the cell. Which of the following supports would be most appropriate and beneficial to the beginning ELLs in the class?

    A. Showing the ELLs a short video on parts of a cell before they perform the task.

    B. Allowing the ELL's to work together on the assessment.

    C. Having ELLs identify parts of a cell orally while referencing a word bank.

    D. Have the ELLs draw a cell and label it.

92. When making testing accommodations for ELLs in a science class, which of the following must the teacher be sure to do?

    A. Give everyone extra time to complete the assessment.

    B. Translate the assessments into the ELLs' home languages.

    C. Provide language dictionaries.

    D. Ensure the standards and constructs tested are consistent with non-ELL assessments.

93. A teacher-made exam is supposed to be assessing student algebra skills. However, the test contains a lot of word problems with long reading passages that contain little math. What might be compromised regarding this test?

    A. Validity

    B. Reliability

    C. Bias

    D. Accountability

94. Ms. Jones is assessing her ESL students' expository writing skills. She has students look at a common picture of the founding fathers writing the Declaration of Independence. She asks students to write two sentences explaining what is happening in the picture. In this case, the teacher has failed to consider:

    A. The students' L2 capabilities

    B. The test's validity

    C. The test's reliability

    D. The test's cultural bias

95. Which of the following assessments would be most effective in measuring an ELL's aural comprehension?

    A. Have students retell a piece of a story they read in class.

    B. Have students read aloud for fluency and measure their correct words per minute.

    C. Have students identify content specific vocabulary in an audio clip.

    D. Have students read a passage and answer multiple-choice questions.

96. An ESL assessment is primarily used to measure:

    A. Students' speaking and listening skills

    B. Students' overall English language skills

    C. Students' reading and writing skills

    D. Students' oral vocabulary skills

97. Which of the following assessment measures speaking, listening, reading, and writing?

    A. Students must take paper strips containing sentences and place them in the proper order: topic sentence, detail 1, detail 2, detail 3, and closing sentence.

    B. Students work in groups to research a topic, discuss the topic, develop a presentation, and deliver a presentation.

    C. Students must fill in the blanks of missing areas of a passage using a word bank provided.

    D. Students must follow a step-by-step recipe the teacher demonstrates where they make omelets: crack the eggs, whisk the eggs, pour the eggs in the pan, cook the eggs, and serve the eggs.

98. Which of the following assessment is considered a cloze exercise?

   A. Students must take paper strips containing sentences and place them in the proper order: topic sentence, detail 1, detail 2, detail 3, and closing sentence.

   B. Students work in groups to research a topic, discuss the topic, develop a presentation, and deliver a presentation.

   C. Students must fill in the blanks of missing areas of a passage using a word bank provided.

   D. Students must follow a step-by-step recipe where they make omelets: crack the eggs, whisk the eggs, pour the eggs in the pan, cook the eggs, and serve the eggs.

99. Which of the following assessment measures the Total Physical Response to language instruction?

   A. Students must take paper strips containing sentences and place them in the proper order: topic sentence, detail 1, detail 2, detail 3, and closing sentence.

   B. Students work in groups to research a topic, discuss the topic, develop a presentation, and deliver a presentation.

   C. Students must fill in the blanks of missing areas of a passage using a word bank provided.

   D. Students must follow a step-by-step recipe where they make omelets: crack the eggs, whisk the eggs, pour the eggs in the pan, cook the eggs, and serve the eggs.

100. Which of the following activity measures writing sequencing?

   A. Students must take paper strips containing sentences and place them in the proper order: topic sentence, detail 1, detail 2, detail 3, and closing sentence.

   B. Students work in groups to research a topic, discuss the topic, develop a presentation, and deliver a presentation.

   C. Students must fill in the blanks of missing areas of a passage using a word bank provided.

   D. Students must follow a step-by-step recipe where they make omelets: crack the eggs, whisk the eggs, pour the eggs in the pan, cook the eggs, and serve the eggs.

101. When a student is an ELL and also qualifies for special education services, which of the following is NOT something that must be provided?

   A. A paraprofessional and interpreter to accompany the student to classes regardless of the student's language acquisition.

   B. Assessments conducted by qualified bilingual evaluators who use culturally valid instruments and procedures appropriate for ELLs and provide accurate data about native language and English language performance.

   C. Use of interpreters for non-English speaking parents during IEP meetings and other important conferences.

   D. Individualized education programs (IEPs) that are culturally and linguistically relevant and that describe how services for English language acquisition and academic instruction will be provided simultaneously.

102. Ms. Helms teaches at a middle school with a population that is predominately Hispanic. According to the Consent Decree, Ms. Helms must do what?

    A. Ensure the comprehensible delivery of instruction to ELL students.

    B. Allow ELL students extra time on quizzes and tests.

    C. Encourage ELLs to speak their home language in class.

    D. Require ELLs speak English only in the classroom.

103. Claudia is an ELL who has been in America for one year. In math class, she is attentive and does well on assignments. In social science class, she is quiet and does not volunteer to read aloud. What can the teacher assume?

    A. Claudia is displaying abnormal development because if she understands the math, she should be volunteering to read in social science class.

    B. Claudia is at a normal stage of language acquisition because math translates across languages, and social science is heavy with English language skills she may not have yet.

    C. Claudia should be speaking in class because a year is plenty of time to become fluent in English.

    D. Claudia may be developmentally delayed in her language skills.

104. High school English students are preparing for the state-mandated assessment. This assessment is high-stakes, and the ESOL teacher knows that many of the ELLs' parents are new to the country and are not familiar with the assessment. Which of the following is the most appropriate first step for the teacher to take to best communicate with the parents?

    A. Post the information about the test on a class website so parents can access it at home.

    B. Send out an email detailing the different aspects of the exam and what to expect on test day.

    C. Arrange for a parent night with interpreters so parents can ask questions about the exam.

    D. Send home a newsletter in the students' home language detailing the aspects of the text.

105. A student has tested out of the ESL program, but he is nervous to leave the ESL program because he knows he will be one of very few people in the mainstream classes with his ethnic background. What can the ELL and mainstream teachers do to help this student?

    A. Insist that the student stay in the ESL program because that is where he is comfortable,

    B. Mainstream the student as quickly as possible so he can get used to the classes.

    C. Allow the student to come back to the ESL program at the end of the month if he still feels uncomfortable.

    D. Allow the student some transition time where he can meet the new teacher, look over some of the assignments, and visit the new class.

106. Zahir is from Pakistan, and she is enrolling in an American public school for the first time. Which of the following can her parents expect to receive?

    A. Home language survey

    B. Placement test results

    C. School ELL data report

    D. The name of an interpreter

107. Within how many days must a school notify parents that their child has been placed in an ESL program?

    A. 5

    B. 10

    C. 20

    D. 30

108. An ELL student is facing suspension for an incident that happened during school. The student and the student's parents are attending a due process hearing regarding the incident. Which of the following must the school provide for the hearing?

    A. An interpreter who is fluent in the student's home language

    B. An interpreter who has knowledge in both languages of any specialized terms or concepts to be used in the communication

    C. An ESOL teacher who knows the student and who can explain the process for the student and parents

    D. It is the parents' responsibility to provide translation services, not the school's responsibility.

109. Which of the following is a two-way bilingual model that is most beneficial to language-minority and language-majority students?

    A. Language-minority students study English independently from language-majority students.

    B. The target language is used as the primary language for all activities throughout the day.

    C. The target language is used for half the language-minority students, while the other half studies content area subjects in their home languages.

    D. Language-minority and language-majority students are integrated in a class in which they receive instruction in both languages.

110. Which of the following circumstances may indicate that an ELL might need testing for special education services?

    A. The student is difficult to understand because of a thick accent.

    B. The student is hesitant to speak in the new language in front of the class.

    C. The student has unusual patterns in L1 as compared to other students using L1.

    D. The student code switches frequently during class discussions.

111. According to research, which of the following is the most effective way to increase student achievement in both L1 and L2?

    A. Time on task in English

    B. At-home practice with parents

    C. Dynamic bilingual education

    D. Scripted bilingual education

112. This is an approach to teaching language or vocabulary through physical movement.

    A. Total Physical Response (TPR)

    B. Cognitive Academic Language Learning Approach (CALLA)

    C. Sheltered Instruction Observation Protocol (SIOP)

    D. Natural Approach

113. This approach rejects formal grammar and mechanics instruction and instead focuses on a stress-free learning environment.

    A. Total Physical Response (TPR)

    B. Cognitive Academic Language Learning Approach (CALLA)

    C. Sheltered Instruction Observation Protocol (SIOP)

    D. Natural Approach

114. This protects English language learners (ELLs) and their right to a free, comprehensible education. It addresses civil and academic rights of ELL students and requires instruction be delivered in a comprehensible manner so ELLs can fully participate.

    A. 504

    B. IDEA

    C. FERPA

    D. The Consent Decree

115. Which of the following practices are most effective when planning for student-led conferences with parents whose first language is not English?

    A. Deliver information in a comprehensible manner.

    B. Allow the student to translate for the parents.

    C. Request a co-teacher translate during the conferences.

    D. Require the student to speak English only during the conference.

116. According to research, which of the following is the best approach to helping students in their second language acquisition?

    A. An abandonment of L1 to focus on L2 only

    B. Language and grammar drills with a focus on L2 vocabulary

    C. Bilingual, differentiated instruction that considers culture and interests and is relevant to students' lives.

    D. English-only immersion with a concentration on conversation and roleplay.

117. This is considered grounded in the classical way of teaching a second language where the focus is on grammar and mechanics, and translation is the most important classroom activity.

    A. Total Physical Response (TPR)

    B. Cognitive Academic Language Learning Approach (CALLA)

    C. Sheltered Instruction Observation Protocol (SIOP)

    D. Grammar-translation

118. This approach uses dialogue and roleplay as its main focus to learning a language.

    A. Sheltered Instruction Observation Protocol (SIOP)

    B. Grammar-translation

    C. Audio-lingual

    D. Total Physical Response (TPR)

119. A group of 15 tenth-grade early ESOL students spend the entire day with the same teacher. This is called the:

    A. Self-contained model

    B. Pull-out model

    C. Inclusion model

    D. Bilingual model

120. Which of the following is considered a best practice when teaching ELLs?

    A. Grammar-translation

    B. Bilingual approach

    C. Self-contained model

    D. Cognitive approach

This page intentionally left blank.

Practice Test 1 Answer Explanations

Number	Answer	Category	Explanation
1	C	Standards-Based Instruction	Answer C contains good words—comprehensible, standards aligned.
2	B	Standards-Based Instruction	Answer choice B is an example of keeping expectations high while accommodating students based on their needs. Scaffolding is a method teachers use to support students with challenging text.
3	A	Standards-Based Instruction	Real world and content area reading are good phrases to be on the lookout for on this exam. Content area alludes to using discipline specific areas (science, math, social studies). Remember the question asks for the MOST effective. Answer A is *most* effective.
4	D	Standards-Based Instruction	The only writing that is used to persuade is D.
5	A	Standards-Based Instruction	Answer A describes a way in which the teacher can activate background knowledge so the students can understand the concepts and apply that to new vocabulary. None of the other answer choices are effective approaches to complex vocabulary pre-reading strategies.
6	C	Standards-Based Instruction	Modeling is a very powerful tool when conveying the importance of appropriate communication. Students look to the teacher for these skills.
7	A	Standards-Based Instruction	The key words here are *most important*. All of the answer choices are pretty good answers, but answer A has to do with differentiated instruction, which is most important here.
8	B	Standards-Based Instruction	Alignment to the standards is key. The focus of this category *is knowledge of standards-based ESOL and content instruction.*
9	D	Standards-Based Instruction	Mastery of standards means that students have a high level of understanding. Because of this, answer D—critical thinking—is the best option.
10	C	Standards-Based Instruction	Integrating all the skills—speaking, listening, reading and writing—is the best way to engage students and help them with second language acquisition.

Number	Answer	Category	Explanation
11	C	Standards-Based Instruction	Heterogeneous groups are formed so that there is a variety of learning levels and student interests. Homogeneous grouping is when students are grouped by the same skill level or reading level. Interest grouping is grouping students based on their interests, which is not indicated in the question. Peer tutoring grouping is a nonsense answer.
12	A	Standards-Based Instruction	Intrinsic motivation is the best answer here. Allowing students to self-select books increases intrinsic motivation. All the other answer choices focus on extrinsic motivators and requirements, which are not as effective as intrinsic motivators.
13	D	Standards-Based Instruction	In this case, choral reading (see reference pages) is most appropriate because in choral reading, students read aloud in unison. Any mistakes are drowned out by the crowd, Also, choral reading helps with momentum and fluency. Silent sustained reading, popcorn reading, and round robin reading are usually never the answers on this type of exam.
14	B	Standards-Based Instruction	These students are reading complex informational text, and the teacher wants them to organize their learning. Therefore, a graphic organizer will help the most here.
15	B	Standards-Based Instruction	Literature circles (see reference pages) are formal cooperative learning activities where students read and analyze text together. Therefore, B is the best answer. Also, we can eliminate whole group and direct instruction (answers A and C) because they are both similar and address the class in its entirety. Individual conferencing to set goals is not related to the task in the question.
16	A	Standards-Based Instruction	Language and culture are intermingled, and it is important that teachers encourage students to use these aspects when thinking about and engaging in writing activities. None of the other answer choices are appropriate for this situation.
17	C	Standards-Based Instruction	Kinesthetic learners prefer to move their bodies during learning. Therefore, answer C is the best choice.
18	A	Standards-Based Instruction	The teacher is allowing students to choose based on multiple intelligences or learning preferences.
19	C	Standards-Based Instruction	Answer C has all the good words related to this competency: *target interventions, flexible grouping, monitor progress*. Answer C also accommodates all learners—proficient and struggling. Answer A pushes the responsibility onto the reading coach, which is usually not the correct answer on this test. Answer B is not differentiated at all. In fact, it lumps everyone together, whether they need interventions or not. Finally, answer D uses homogenous grouping in a bad way; the struggling readers are doing work while the on-level readers get to choose their activities. This is not the most effective approach.

Think Like a Test Maker

Number	Answer	Category	Explanation
20	D	Standards-Based Instruction	Because the student scores well on the tests and quizzes, we can assume the student has mastered the concepts and standards but is unmotivated to complete the classwork and assignments. In this case, we want to be on the lookout for an answer choice where the teacher and the student find a solution by increasing intrinsic motivation for the student. Allowing the student to choose activities increases autonomy, a component of intrinsic motivation. Answer choices A, B and C all highlight extrinsic rewards. While extrinsic rewards work in the short term, they will not be sustainable over time.
21	A	Foundation of Linguistics	Phonological awareness is putting phonemic awareness and phonics together. Remember, phonological awareness is the umbrella, and phonics and phonemic awareness fall under that umbrella. Structural analysis is not related in this situation.
22	C	Foundation of Linguistics	Phonemic awareness involves only listening to and pronouncing sounds in words. In fact, students can practice phonemic awareness without any paper or pencils. It is only the individual sounds (phonemes) in words.
23	D	Foundation of Linguistics	The students are manipulating the word by switching or substituting one sound for another. This is considered the highest level of phonemic awareness.
24	A	Foundation of Linguistics	Segmenting is breaking apart a word by individual sounds (phonemes). This helps students with phonemic awareness. Answers B and D are exercises in morphology. Segmenting is the opposite of blending, which eliminates answer C.
25	B	Foundation of Linguistics	Onset is the beginning consonant and consonant cluster. Rime is the vowel and consonants that follow. In this case, the only answer choice with a definitive onset and rime is B. The /t/ is the onset. The /ap/ is the rime. The other answer choices are broken up by syllables, not onset and rime.
26	B	Foundation of Linguistics	Because the student is in the partial-alphabetic stage, the student only knows some of the letters. The next step would be to work on medial sounds or the middle /u/ vowel sound.
27	D	Foundation of Linguistics	Environmental print is the print of everyday life. By labeling all the everyday objects in the room, the teacher is helping students with their environmental print.
28	D	Foundation of Linguistics	Even though it is just scribble, the student is displaying an essential skill in beginning reading, which is distinguishing between pictures (stick figure) and text (scribble).
29	A	Foundation of Linguistics	This activity helps with alphabetic principle because students will understand that speech can be represented in print, which is part of the alphabetic principle.

Number	Answer	Category	Explanation
30	D	Foundation of Linguistics	In the English language, some words do not follow all phonological rules. Therefore, teaching phonological generalizations is best because there will always be exceptions to the rules.
31	D	Foundation of Linguistics	Semantic cueing is when students use meaning around the word (pictures, other words, etc.) to figure out the word.
32	A	Foundation of Linguistics	Diphthongs are sounds formed by the combination of two vowels in a single syllable, in which the sound begins as one vowel and moves toward another. They can appear in the initial, middle, or final position in a word. Words like *aisle*, *join*, and *loud* contain diphthongs.
33	A	Foundation of Linguistics	Memorizing high frequency words is the best way to increase automatic word recognition.
34	B	Foundation of Linguistics	Answer B is decoding because the student is reading (decoding), and coin is a word that uses a vowel team (oi). Remember, encoding is when a student hears a word and writes it down (spelling test). Therefore, eliminate anything that is encoding—Answers A and C. A vowel team is a syllable that has two consecutive vowels. This eliminates answer D, because bake and back would be an error in CVCe and CVCC words.
35	C	Foundation of Linguistics	Answers A and B are students who are not ready for phonics. They need to be in the phonemic awareness stage of learning. Answer C is a good candidate for explicit phonics instruction because the student needs help with words that are in text often (medium frequency words). The last student in answer D is above explicit phonics instruction because the only trouble the student is having is with academic specific words—mitochondria, electoral college, literature.
36	B	Foundation of Linguistics	For students to be ready for phonics instruction, they need to be able to identify blends in words and to segment words into different parts. All of the other answer choices describe students who are in the beginning or middle of phonemic awareness and are not ready for phonics.
37	D	Foundation of Linguistics	Decoding, fluency, and reading comprehension (in that order) are interrelated. A student must have all three skills to be a proficient reader. Before a student can have fluency, the student must be able to decode. Before the student can have comprehension, the student must have fluency.
38	C	Foundation of Linguistics	C stands for consonant. V stands for vowel. The small e stands for silent e. The word *mate* is a CVCe word. *Crank* is a CCVCC word. *Mat* is a CVC word. The word *believe* does not fit here.

Number	Answer	Category	Explanation
39	C	Foundation of Linguistics	High-frequency words are sight words and should be memorized. Sight words occur frequently in the text, and some do not follow the rules of phonics. It is most effective for students to memorize these words rather than trying to decode them or sound them out.
40	See Table	Foundation of Linguistics	
41	A	Foundation of Linguistics	It is important to keep in mind developmentally appropriate practices here. The students are in 3rd grade and are learning about English syntax. Therefore, understanding that a sentence contains a subject and a predicate is best for this situation. Answer B is too advanced for these students. Answer C is about phonics. Answer D outlines morphology.
42	A	Foundation of Linguistics	The general rule is to stress the second-to-last syllable of words that end in *tion* or *sion*. The big dot represents the stressed syllable.
43	A	Foundations of Language Acquisition	A. **Acquisition-learning hypothesis** – students develop their linguistic skills through acquisition and learning. In some cases, acquisition is more important than learning. B. **Monitor hypothesis** – the practical result of learned grammar. This is when students start to correct themselves based on the language rules. C. **Input hypothesis** – language progression happens when they comprehend language input (conversation, writing) that is slightly more advanced. It is usually explained as i+1 (input plus 1). D. **Affective filter hypothesis** – motivation, self-confidence, anxiety, and personal traits all affect language acquisition. E. **Natural order hypothesis** – Understanding that grammar in language follows a natural order.

For item 40, the table matches Skills to Activities:

Skill	Activity
Compound sentences	Using conjunctions to join clauses.
Modal verbs	Placing words like should, could, and must properly in a sentence
Topic sentence and supporting details	Organizing sentences in a logical order
Speaking and listening	Roleplay

Number	Answer	Category	Explanation
44	B	Foundations of Language Acquisition	**Monitor hypothesis** – the practical result of learned grammar. This is when students start to correct themselves based on the language rules.
45	B	Foundations of Language Acquisition	A. **Overgeneralization** – extending the application of a rule to items that are excluded from it. For example, using the ed for past tense for every verb (I *sleeped* instead of *slept*). B. **Circumlocution** – defining the concept of a word or topic without saying the correct word. This happens in early stages of language acquisition. C. **Simplification** – this is a nonsense answer in this question. D. **Affect filter** – has to do with motivation and does not fit this question.
46	D	Foundations of Language Acquisition	**Overgeneralization** - extending the application of a rule to items that are excluded from it. For example, using the *ed* for past tense for every verb (I *sleeped* instead of *slept*).
47	C	Foundations of Language Acquisition	Pay attention to words and phrases in the question stem. In this case, the question asks about two languages. That should point to answer C—dual (two) immersion. This means that the students are immersed in both languages. This is a characteristic of bilingual education and is considered a good word or phrase to look for in the correct answer choices.
48	A	Foundations of Language Acquisition	The terms *high expectations* and *standards* are good words and phrases to be on the lookout for on this exam. If you see them in an answer choice, they are probably the correct answer.
49	A	Foundations of Language Acquisition	Whenever possible, select answer choices that showcase bilingual education. Bilingual education is one of the most important concepts on this test. All the other answer choices in this item are considered non-answers. Avoid these answers on the exam.
50	C	Foundations of Language Acquisition	These students are using BICS in this scenario. *BICS* means basic interpersonal communication skills and is what students use in their conversational language. *CAPLS* means standards for cognitive academic language proficiency and has to do with academic language. The other two answer choices do not fit here.
51	B	Foundations of Language Acquisition	**Interlanguage** – the process of learning a second language (L2) is characteristically non-linear and fragmentary, marked by a mixed landscape of rapid progression in certain areas but slow movement, incubation, or even permanent stagnation in others.

Number	Answer	Category	Explanation
52	D	Foundations of Language Acquisition	These students are receiving explicit academic instruction in the content area to strengthen academic skills. A. **Immersion** – immersing students in L2 classes B. **Bilingual** – Using both L1 and L2 in classroom instruction C. **Cooperative** – this is when students work together in groups. D. **Sheltered** – providing meaningful instruction in the content areas (social studies, math, science) for transitioning limited English proficiency (LEP) students toward higher academic achievement while they reach English fluency.
53	A	Foundations of Language Acquisition	Students who thrive with moving their bodies and using hands-on activities are kinesthetic learners.
54	D	Foundations of Language Acquisition	Chunking is the best approach here because it keeps standards high but also scaffolds for the student who may need supports because she is just exiting the ESOL program. None of the other answer choices are as effective.
55	A	Foundations of Language Acquisition	When a teacher lowers the affective filter, the teacher lowers the frustration level, and the student feels more comfortable and motivated. The teacher can do this with positive feedback, encouraging the students to take risks, and developing a safe place in the classroom for students to try reading in L2.
56	C	Foundations of Language Acquisition	Often, drawing a picture or using graphics is the best way to help explain concepts of another language. In this case, translating the idiom will not work because idioms are language specific, and this may cause more confusion. Looking up the idiom is also unproductive because idioms are not phases easily defined in a dictionary. Finally, skipping over the idiom does not help the student learn the idiomatic phrase.
57	A	Foundations of Language Acquisition	Activating background knowledge is the best way to help ELLs tackle difficult text. Because students struggle with the text, understanding what the text is about first will help reduce confusion.
58	C	Foundations of Language Acquisition	During early stages of language acquisition, visual representations are always good practice. Drawing the life cycle of the frog is the best option for this situation.
59	C	Foundations of Language Acquisition	The student is editing himself which is part of Krashen's monitor hypothesis.

Number	Answer	Category	Explanation
60	D	Foundations of Language Acquisition	Answer D allows the student to develop oral language, reading, and listening skills.
61	D	Cultural Awareness	Additive bilingualism occurs when an ELL has no loss of the primary language and the associated culture.
62	B	Cultural Awareness	Sociolinguistics is concerned with language in social and cultural context, especially how people with different social identities, such as gender, age, race, ethnicity, class, speak and how their speech changes in different situations. This would be the most appropriate professional development for teachers wanting to be culturally responsive.
63	A	Cultural Awareness	Because the student is abandoning the traditional culture, the student is assimilating. This can be traumatic for parents. The student wants to fit in with peers, but the family wants to continue traditions and customs. A better balance is acculturation, where the student merges the two cultures—adopting some new practices while keeping traditions.
64	C	Cultural Awareness	The best thing the teacher can do to make the student feel comfortable is to meet with the student privately and welcome him. The teacher should also go over the classroom routines, so the student knows what to do each day. The student is most likely scared and uncomfortable. Therefore, having the student introduce himself to the entire class is inappropriate. Meeting with the student's parents is not going to help in the immediate situation. In addition, grouping ELLs together so they can translate for each other is bad practice and not inclusive.
65	D	Cultural Awareness	The most culturally responsive action in all of the choices is Answer D. Allowing students to use their home language when needed is always a good answer. In addition, encouraging students to identify situations in their own culture that go with the reading is effective in activating background knowledge.
66	C	Cultural Awareness	Fossilization occurs when the ELL is immersed in an ESL environment and lives in a linguistically insular community.
67	B	Cultural Awareness	In this case, the teacher must investigate further to see if the student's stuttering is a result of navigating the new to the language, or if this is an issue in L1 also. If she also stutters in L1, then the teacher can request an evaluation. However, going with answer A first is jumping ahead a bit. None of the other answer choices are appropriate.

Number	Answer	Category	Explanation
68	A	Cultural Awareness	The social interactionist perspective views social interaction as playing a critical role in the learning process. Learners are provided opportunities to construct new language through socially mediated interactions in the classroom. That is why roleplay is such a good activity for this situation.
69	B	Cultural Awareness	Small groups are safe spaces for students to discuss their cultural traditions. In addition, the teacher encourages students to ask questions, which further adds to the activity and helps students feel good about themselves and others.
70	C	Cultural Awareness	Pragmatics are social cues in language that a social linguist would be most interested in studying.
71	A	Cultural Awareness	This represents the interrelatedness between culture and language.
72	D	Cultural Awareness	In teacher-centered schools, the teacher leads the class while students exclusively listen. These students may be used to this method where they are from.
73	A	Cultural Awareness	Answer A includes culturally responsive practices.
74	A	Cultural Awareness	If the teacher is assessing sequencing, then the student should be able to show mastery by telling her the sequence. Oral assessments are an effective accommodation for ELL students.
75	D	Cultural Awareness	Regardless of language, ability, exceptionality, or level, the state standards should always be the first thing a teacher references when planning instruction.
76	C	Cultural Awareness	Integrative motivation refers to a learner's intrinsic orientation or desire to communicate with, be more like, or to join the L2 (second or foreign language) user community
77	C	Cultural Awareness	The teacher is trying to minimize context-reduced situations in biology class, meaning the teacher wants to provide more context to complicated subject matter. Often in classes like science and social science, lecture, papers, and tests are the norm. However, those approaches do not provide context for complex academic language. Therefore, having students work in groups to discuss the concepts would help to increase context and make it easier for ELLs to understand these complex concepts in English.
78	B	Cultural Awareness	One of the biggest intrinsic motivators for students learning a second language is to be able to communicate with peers.

Number	Answer	Category	Explanation
79	A	Cultural Awareness	Hand gestures mean different things in different cultures. For example, using your pointer finger to summon someone is very insulting to some people. In many countries, that gesture is used for dogs only. Therefore, when teaching ELLs, it is important to research common hand gestures and what they mean in other cultures.
80	D	Cultural Awareness	This question is tricky because all the answer choices sound reasonable. Let's eliminate them one by one. Answer A includes setting goals *for* students. This can be eliminated because when the teacher sets the goals, that is the opposite of student-centered. Eliminate answer B and C because, while they contain effective practices, they are not necessarily culturally responsive. Answer D is not only best practice but also culturally responsive because the methods provide a safe space to acquire a new language. In addition, this answer choice mentions high standards, which is also student-centered and culturally responsive. Teachers should always keep academic standards high while supporting and scaffolding for students.
81	C	Assessment	Criterion-referenced exams measure the standards, which is the criteria of the exam. Norm-referenced assessments use a percentile to compare students to other students.
82	B	Assessment	A. **Internal Validity** – The study was conducted properly, and results can be applied within the context of the study. B. **External Validity** – Results can be generalized to the outside world. C. **Accuracy** – Precision of results (nonsense answer for this problem) D. **Reliability** – Consistency of the measure (results are consistent when the test is administered again and again).
83	D	Assessment	**Reliability** - The consistency of the measure (results are consistent when the test is administered again and again).
84	D	Assessment	When students have mastered the standards, they can apply their knowledge to higher-order thinking activities. Out of all the answer choices, the higher-order thinking activities listed are research papers, presentations, and formal debates. Also, never use homework to assess expertise or mastery; homework is for practice. This eliminates answers A and B. Finally, checklists and surveys in answer choice C do not measure expertise.
85	A	Assessment	Using a variety of assessments will provide many forms of data. When the teacher sees consistencies in that data, the teacher can assume the data is reliable. Answer choices C and D use strong language—*only*—and limit data collection. Teachers should not rely solely on the textbook for assessment.

Number	Answer	Category	Explanation
86	B	Assessment	Rubrics are used to set expectations and serve as a checklist for student projects, especially writing projects. Rubrics are helpful for both the teacher and student to measure skills and complete tasks.
87	C	Assessment	A diagnostic assessment helps the teacher to diagnose deficits in students' skills. The other options are not effective for this situation.
88	C	Assessment	More time is the most common accommodation for ELLs. Also, pay attention to the term *intermediate* ELLs in the question stem. If they are intermediate, answers A, B, and D are not appropriate for intermediate ELLs.
89	D	Assessment	Portfolios show progress over time and include samples of student work. They are the most effective tool here.
90	B	Assessment	Formative assessments are ongoing and are used to monitor progress.
91	C	Assessment	Oral assessments are usually effective modifications for ELLs. In addition, the word bank will support the ELLs with exposure to the possible words needed to label the cell. However, this also assesses the students' knowledge.
92	D	Assessment	While the teacher may make accommodations for students who are ELL, the standards and constructs do not change. The ELLs should be tested on the same material as their non-ELL peers.
93	A	Assessment	In this case, the test is not assessing what it is intended to assess. Therefore, the validity might be compromised.
94	D	Assessment	The assessment contains cultural bias because the picture is specific to United States history. The teacher should have used a neutral image so that all students can understand what is happening in the picture.
95	C	Assessment	Aural has to do with the ear or hearing. Therefore, to measure aural comprehension, a listening assessment is most effective. Therefore, answer C is the correct answer.
96	B	Assessment	The purpose of a proficiency test in an ESL class is to get a snapshot of learners' overall ability in English.
97	B	Assessment	A research project and presentation completed in cooperative groups hits all the communication skills, both receptive and expressive.
98	C	Assessment	A cloze activity is a fill in the bank and assesses comprehension and word recognition skills.

Number	Answer	Category	Explanation
99	D	Assessment	Total Physical Response (TPR) is a method of teaching language or vocabulary concepts by using physical movement to react to verbal input. In this case, the teacher uses a recipe to elicit a TPR.
100	A	Assessment	Constructing a paragraph by putting sentences in order is assessing sequencing.
101	A	Advocating for ELLs	Answer B, C, and D are all required for students with disabilities and who are ELL. Paraprofessionals are not required for every student. If a student needs a paraprofessional, one will be provided. However, these services are based on need.
102	A	Advocating for ELLs	The Consent Decree provides a structure that ensures the delivery of the comprehensible instruction to which ELL students are entitled. The phrase *comprehensible instruction* means that teachers will use accommodations, ancillary materials, like Spanish to English resources, and other methods to help students with English Language Acquisition.
103	B	Advocating for ELLs	Math does not require a significant amount of language acquisition. However, English class does. Since Claudia has only been in the country a year, this is normal in the language acquisition process.
104	C	Advocating for ELLs	Answer C is the best option. Inviting parents to come to the school and having interpreters present is key to getting parents' questions answered. It also forms trust between the parents and the school. Answer D is okay, but answer C is best.
105	D	Advocating for ELLs	A period of transition is important for an ELL who has exited out of an ESL program. This period will help the ELL acclimate to changes in classes, peers, teachers, and expectations.
106	A	Advocating for ELLs	When an ELL enrolls in school, parents should receive a home language survey or similar form to fill out that helps the school identify potential English learners who are eligible for language assistance services.
107	D	Advocating for ELLs	If your child is identified as an English learner, the school must notify you in writing within 30 days of the school year starting with information about your child's English language proficiency level, programs and services available to meet your child's educational needs, and your right to opt your child out of a program or particular services for English learners.
108	B	Advocating for ELLs	According to the U.S. Department of Justice, school districts should ensure that interpreters and translators have knowledge in both languages of any specialized terms or concepts to be used in the communication at issue, and are trained on the role of an interpreter and translator, the ethics of interpreting and translating, and the need to maintain confidentiality.

Number	Answer	Category	Explanation
109	D	Advocating for ELLs	Answer D describes two-way bilingual education and is beneficial for language-minority and language majority students according to research.
110	C	Advocating for ELLs	Answers A, B, and D are all normal actions ELLs take when learning a new language. However, unusual patterns in L1 as compared to others may indicate the student needs additional special education services, and testing would be the proper next step.
111	C	Advocating for ELLs	Remember, if you see *bilingual education* in an answer choice, look closely. First, eliminate A and B because *bilingual education* is a good phrase for this test. That leaves C and D. A dynamic curriculum is one that is differentiated and adaptive. Scripted curriculum is very limited. Therefore, C is the best answer.
112	A	Advocating for ELLs	A. **TPR** – stands for Total Physical Response and uses movement to teach language and vocabulary. It mimics the way infants use language. B. **CALLA** – stands for the cognitive academic language learning approach and consists of metacognitive, cognitive and social strategies C. **SIOP** – stands for Sheltered Instruction Observation Protocol and involves eight components: 1. Lesson Preparation 2. Building Background 3. Comprehensible Input 4. Strategies 5. Interaction 6. Practice/Application 7. Lesson Delivery 8. Review & Assessment D. **Natural Approach** – little focus on grammar. Learning environment is positive, and students have the opportunity to spontaneously engage in L2.
113	D	Advocating for ELLs	**Natural Approach** has little focus on grammar. The learning environment is positive, and students have the opportunity to spontaneously engage in L2.

Number	Answer	Category	Explanation
114	D	Advocating for ELLs	**The Consent Decree.** Grounded in the 14th Amendment and the result of League of United Latin American Citizens (LULAC) vs. State Board of Education, the Consent Decree protects English Language Learners (ELL) and their right to a free, comprehensible education. It addresses civil and academic rights of ELL students and requires that instruction be delivered in a comprehensible manner so ELLs can fully participate. Since 1975, federal law has required that students with disabilities have access to school and a free appropriate public education.
115	A	Advocating for ELLs	The term *comprehensible* is a good word to look for in the answer choices on this part of the test. It has to do with the Consent Decree and parent and student rights. It means that the school does everything it can to help students and parents understand (comprehend) their education.
116	C	Advocating for ELLs	Answer C has all the good words (*bilingual*, *differentiated*, *culture*, *interest*, *relevance*) when it comes to ESOL instruction. Look for these words in the answer choices when moving through this exam. All of the other answer choices allude to an English-only approach which is usually not the correct answer on this test.
117	D	Advocating for ELLs	Grammar-translation focuses on the mechanics of a language and the students' ability to translate the language.
118	C	Advocating for ELLs	The audio-lingual approach focuses on the speaking and listening part of learning a language.
119	A	Advocating for ELLs	When students spend the whole day in one class, this is called a self-contained classroom.
120	B	Advocating for ELLs	According to research, bilingual education beats out all of the others listed in the answer choices.

1. According to WIDA standards which of the following is most important?

   A. Students must be immersed in the second language as soon as possible.

   B. Standards must be high for all students and implemented in an equitable manner.

   C. Students must work to abandon the first language so they can learn the second language.

   D. Standards must focus on language acquisition before content area knowledge.

2. A teacher has several ELLs in class and wants to provide the best learning environment for the students. To ensure this, which the following should the teacher practice daily?

   A. Engage students in roleplay activities so they can increase their conversational English proficiency.

   B. Group students based on English language proficiency and administer interventions to students who need them.

   C. Assign at-home practice so students can involve their parents in second language acquisition and learning.

   D. Provide students with multiple opportunities to practice learner autonomy and take responsibility for their learning.

3. A student who is in early production would best benefit from which of the following?

   A. Graphic representations of everyday situations.

   B. Novels depicting everyday life.

   C. Standardized reading passages and comprehension questions.

   D. Multiple-choice tests with simple language.

4. Which of the following would be considered student-centered learning for ELLs?

   A. Allowing students to decide what they learn

   B. Allowing students to work in groups

   C. Considering students' learning preferences

   D. Considering students' reading levels

5. Which of the following would be most effective in communicating what ELLs are responsible for learning by the end of a lesson?

   A. Communicating measurable objectives

   B. Communicating expectations for assignment grades.

   C. Having a rubric for cooperative learning

   D. Pairing students based on interest for roleplay activities.

6. When planning instruction for ELLs, what should the teacher do first?

    A. Enlist the help of the paraprofessional who can translate assignments.

    B. Consult the state-adopted academic standards for the content area taught.

    C. Allow students to work as partners to help each other translate.

    D. Observe another ELL teacher who has more experience.

7. A teacher is working with ELLs and explaining that in different parts of the United States, people pronounce words differently and even call objects by different names. For example, she shows a picture of a soft drink and explains that some people call this *soda* while others call this *pop*. What is the teacher explaining?

    A. Register

    B. Language acquisition

    C. Dialect

    D. Assimilation

8. A content-area teacher has several ELLs in class who are in the beginning stages of language acquisition. The class will be doing a spelling test. Which of the following would be most effective in differentiating instruction based on students' levels of language acquisition?

    A. Allowing students to sit out of the spelling test if they are not ready

    B. Having other students who are more fluent translate for the ELLs

    C. Have the students spell words that are easier than what is on the standard spelling test

    D. Provide students with a word bank or words that are partially spelled to scaffold the activity

9. A content-area teacher with several ELLs wants to help students understand their stages of learning. Which of the following would be most effective?

    A. Weekly multiple-choice tests

    B. Self-assessments after each lesson

    C. Spelling tests for new words

    D. Partner reading of new text

10. A teacher is helping ELLs with their reading comprehension. The standard for the lesson is students will use metacognition to increase comprehension and critical thinking of informational text. Which of the following activities would be most effective in this situation?

    A. Predicting and questioning activities during reading

    B. Labeling a graphic organizer for text elements before reading

    C. Working in cooperative groups to discuss text

    D. Using comprehension worksheets to tests students understanding

Think Like a Test Maker

11. A science teacher has several students who are kinesthetic learners. The teacher wants to be sure to consider this when planning the next lesson. Which of the following would be most effective for students who are kinesthetic learners?

    A. Cooperative learning to discuss science concepts

    B. Interest grouping so students can engage with content they like

    C. Roleplay centers where students act out different relevant scenarios

    D. Comprehension exercises for a new novel the class is reading

12. According to the standards for an upcoming lesson, students will need to use their receptive and productive skills to understand content-area text. Which of the following activities would NOT accomplish this? Choose TWO.

    A. Students will read a passage and write an essay about the passage.

    B. Students will listen to a story read to them and then retell the important parts.

    C. Students will either complete a task through an oral presentation or a writing assignment.

    D. Students will engage in roleplay where one student listens while the other student speaks.

13. Which of the following is most important when educating ELLs in a content area classroom?

    A. Use standards in tandem with culturally responsive teaching practices.

    B. Allow students to work in groups until they are comfortable speaking aloud.

    C. Expect that ELLs will remain behind their peers academically for at least one year.

    D. Implement English-only practices so students are immersed in the language.

14. One of the objectives for a biology lesson on cells and the body is to use background knowledge to understand new concepts. Which of the following can the teacher do to support ELLs and all students in the classroom regarding this objective? Choose TWO.

    A. Have students work in literature circles to discuss the text while reading.

    B. Show a short video before reading that explains some of the complex concepts in the text.

    C. Allow students to use a dictionary to look up unfamiliar words.

    D. Pre-teach difficult academic vocabulary before reading the text.

    E. Allow students to choose how they will show mastery of the standards.

15. Which of the following is most important to consider when drafting lesson objectives for ELLs in a content area class?

    A. Are the objectives easy enough for the ELLs who may struggle?

    B. Do the objectives have opportunities for students to speak English often?

    C. Are the objectives measurable and culturally relevant?

    D. Will ELLs be able to understand the objectives before the lesson?

16. An ESL teacher is working with students on their independent reading. The ELL students are at various reading levels. What would be the benefit of using an online reading program in this situation? Choose TWO.

    A. The students are more engaged when reading online.

    B. The online program automatically measures students' level and adjusts accordingly.

    C. The teacher can capture reading data on students quickly and efficiently and make decisions.

    D. Having students read on the computer reduces the number of books needed in the classroom.

    E. Having students read on the computer gives the teacher time to work with others who may be at low levels.

17. Which of the following is considered register?

    A. An ELL says to a classmate, "What's up?"

    B. An ELL uses a dictionary to look up words.

    C. An ELL tells the teacher, "I no go on bus today."

    D. An ELL says, "I want the pencil azul."

18. Which of the following activities would be most beneficial to increasing students' listening comprehension?

    A. Have the students read a story to another student and have the student who did not read retell the important parts back to the students who did and then switch roles.

    B. Have students read a story and answer comprehension questions about the story orally.

    C. Have students work in cooperative groups to read and discuss the story.

    D. Have students roleplay a real-world scenario about a grocery store.

19. Which of the following would impact an ELL student negatively?

    A. Holding the student to high academic standards and objectives.

    B. Limiting the student's exposure to difficult words until the student has proficiency in L2.

    C. Allowing students to work in groups when reading a passage from the textbook.

    D. Allowing the student to use L1 when needed while learning L2.

20. A teacher wants to increase students' critical thinking skills. Which of the following should the teacher do first?

    A. Have students speak in English only.

    B. Have students use graphic organizers to categorize thought processes.

    C. Allow students to think critically in L1 and L2.

    D. Have students work with other ELLs to discuss complex concepts.

21. Which of the following is not part of the Universal Language Principles?

    A. Language is rule-governed

    B. Language is systematic

    C. Language is arbitrary

    D. Language is logical

22. Which of the following shows the correct stress syllable in the word *exceptional*?

    A. ●●⬤●

    B. ●⬤●●

    C. ●●●⬤

    D. ⬤●●●

23. An ESOL teacher is working with students on pronunciation. She has students say the word *back* and the word *jab*. She focuses on the /b/ sound. The b sound is different in the *back* than it is in the word *jab*. Which of the following is the teacher working on?

    A. Intonation

    B. Syllabication

    C. Voice vs. voiceless sounds

    D. Dialect patterns

24. An ELL is working on the -ed at the end of words. When asked, the ELL believes the letter at the end of the word walk*ed* is walk*t*. Why might the student think this?

    A. If a past-tense verb ends in an unvoiced consonant, the -ed sounds like -t.

    B. If a past-tense verb ends in in a voiced consonant, the -ed sounds like a -t.

    C. When the verb is stressed at the end of the word, it sounds like a -t.

    D. When the verb is not stressed at the end of the word, it sounds like a -t.

25. An ESL teacher is working with students on how different verbs can help the sentence with importance or necessity. The teacher is using the sentence below.

    She <u>couldn't</u> possibly tell her father about the D she received on her exam.

    Which of the following is the teacher working on?

    A. Adverbs

    B. Modal verbs

    C. Adjectives

    D. Contractions

26. A student says, "John, which is my friend, came over to my house yesterday." This student would benefit from which of the following supports?

A. Explicit instruction in relative pronouns

B. Explicit instruction in possessive pronouns

C. Explicit instruction in complex sentences

D. Explicit instruction phonemic awareness

27. Which of the following would be most appropriate in helping ELL students who struggle with phonetics?

A. Explicit instruction in high frequency word recognition.

B. Explicit instruction in digraphs, consonant blends, and vowel teams

C. Explicit instruction in reading aloud in class

D. Explicit instruction in writing complex sentences.

28. The following excerpt was taken from an intermediate ELL's writing sample about winter break.

My family and me went beach. It was cold. No matter. We had fun. We were together. Holiday vacation at my grandmother house.

Which of the following supports would help this student improve her writing in English?

A. Word choice

B. Sentence structure

C. Word order

D. Spelling

29. During a spelling test, some beginning ELLs spell the following words. What strategy are they using while spelling?

Target Word	Spelling
phone	fone
beach	bech
could	cud
hook	huk

A. The students are spelling using phonics.

B. The students are spelling using semantics.

C. The students are spelling using alliteration.

D. The students are spelling using phonemic awareness.

30. A teacher is working with intermediate ELLs on their writing. The teacher wants students to connect sentences in a way that give variance and flow to their writing. What should the teacher focus on?

   A. Syntax

   B. Transitions

   C. Semantics

   D. Spelling

31. Which of the following should an ELL teacher focus on when working with ELLs on their writing?

   A. Writing should be grammatically correct and contain few errors.

   B. Writing is expressive and should not be bound by grammatical rules.

   C. Writing is best when workshopped in groups and peer reviewed.

   D. Writing should be a reciprocal process and focus should be on revision.

32. Which of the following student sentences contains an error in punctuation?

   A. She went to the store and bought a new dress.

   B. She went to the store and she bought a new dress.

   C. While at the store, she bought a new dress.

   D. She went to the store because she needed a new dress.

33. This is the study of the smallest units of meaning in words. Teachers use this to help students break apart compound words and analyze their meaning.

   A. Phonemic awareness

   B. Phonics

   C. Morphology

   D. Alphabetic principle

34. An ESL teacher is explaining to beginning ELLs that in English, we do not always fully pronounce vowel sounds in words. In many words, the vowel sounds are short and lazy. Which of the following concepts is she teaching?

   A. Morphology

   B. Phonemic awareness

   C. Schwa

   D. Intonation

35. An ELL teacher is having students put their fingers gently on their throats while saying words like *bed*, *said*, *lead*. She is having them focus on the ending d sound in the words. What skill is the teacher working on with ELLs?

   A. Stress patterns

   B. Phonemic awareness

   C. Phonics

   D. Voice and voiceless sounds

36. An ELL teacher is working on free morphemes. Which word would be best to use for this lesson?

   A. closely

   B. happily

   C. station

   D. easily

37. An ESL teacher is working with students on trigraphs. Which of the following sets of words would be most appropriate?

   A. catch, weight, bright

   B. soon, balloon, Halloween

   C. camera, valet, scone

   D. make, take, bake

38. Which of the following sentences would be most effective in working with ELLs on compound sentences?

   A. While waiting for the bus, she read her book.

   B. She waited for the bus, and she read her book.

   C. She read her book as she waited for the bus.

   D. She waited for the bus and read her book.

39. An ELL student writes the following sentence below. What can be assumed when looking at the sentence?

   I slept through the night. My sister waked me up before my alarm goed off.

   A. The student needs support in phonics.

   B. The student needs support in phonemic awareness.

   C. The student is overgeneralizing past-tense rules.

   D. The student does not understand punctuation.

40. Which of the following would be the most effective way to provide students with opportunities to build and extend their phonics skills in a variety of ways?

   A. Have students use dictionaries to identify parts of speech and spelling.

   B. Allow students to work with their friends when speaking English in conversation.

   C. Use chunks of text so students can read fluently.

   D. Use carefully sequenced decodable texts to progressively incorporate letter–sound relationships.

Think Like a Test Maker

41. A new teacher has several ELLs in science class. The teacher wants to be sure the students receive a comprehensible education. Which of the following is the most important thing to consider for the ELLs?

   A. Seating the students in the front of the class because the students need to be able to hear and understand what the teacher is saying.

   B. Helping students memorize words commonly used in the English language so they can focus on more complex skills of language acquisition.

   C. Providing opportunities for students to engage in meaningful social interaction and dialogue so students can begin to use English in relevant settings.

   D. Allowing students to work with peers who speak the same first language so the ELLs feel comfortable in class.

42. Which of the following most accurately outlines schools' responsibilities once an ELL has exited an ESL or ESOL program?

   A. The student will be mainstreamed and no longer monitored after exiting the ESL or ESOL program.

   B. The student will still have some classes in an ESL or ESOL program to support language acquisition.

   C. The student must score proficient on state-mandated reading tests within the first two years of exiting the program.

   D. The student will be monitored for two years after meeting the state requirements and exiting the ESL or ESOL program.

43. Which of the following is accurate regarding students' second language acquisition and how teachers can support students who are ELL?

   A. Cognitive development in L1 should be discontinued when developing L2.

   B. Cognitive development in L1 should only be a priority when educating elementary students.

   C. Cognitive development in L1 should be the priority over cognitive development in L2.

   D. Cognitive development in L2 should take place while supporting cognitive development in L1.

44. Which of the following can a teacher do if the teacher is using the comprehensible input hypothesis?

   A. Provide second language learners an environment that is low anxiety and a safe place to speak L2.

   B. Provide students with a paraprofessional to interpret the teacher's classroom instruction when needed.

   C. Seat the ELLs next to each other so they feel comfortable speaking L2 during class discussions.

   D. Recommend ELLs be monitored for special education in case they have any learning disabilities.

45. An ESL teacher is having ELLs talk to each other about their weekend. A Spanish-speaking student says to another, "I went to the beach pretty." This is an example of:

   A. Code switching

   B. Language interference

   C. Language convergence

   D. Back channeling

46. A middle school ESL teacher is working with students on the different ways in which they speak to teachers and their peers. Which of the following activities would be most effective in this situation?

    A. Have students listen to different conversations and identify different registers.

    B. Have students read about the norms in communication in the English language.

    C. Have students roleplay different scenarios using different registers for each situation.

    D. Have students write down formal and informal words used in language.

47. A fifth-grade ELL student is having trouble with basic phonics and phonemic awareness. Which of the following might be contributing to the lack of skills?

    A. The student is in the wrong grade level and needs to be tested for a disability.

    B. The student may have had limited or interrupted formal education in the first language.

    C. The student is speaking the first language at home and is unable to progress.

    D. The student needs the support of a paraprofessional to translate into the student's L1.

48. Which of the following is important for ESL and general education teachers to remember when teaching ELLs?

    A. ELLs will often stay behind their peers in reading and math.

    B. ELLs should be given extra time to complete assignments.

    C. ELLs should be held to high expectations in the classroom.

    D. ELLs should speak English as much as possible in school.

49. Che is an ELL who is progressing quickly in his reading and writing in L2. However, he does not interact much with other students in class, and his conversational English is not as strong as his written English. What can the teacher do to help Che?

    A. Have Che listen to conversations in an audio learning center.

    B. Incorporate roleplay of social interactions into Che's classroom assignments.

    C. Have Che speak English at home with his parents.

    D. Require Che to speak English only when speaking in class.

50. Which of the following would help ELLs who are developing oral language in L2?

    A. Listen centers

    B. Reading centers

    C. Speaking centers

    D. Writing centers

51. Which of the following is most accurate regarding acquiring proficiency in a second language?

    A. Support in L1 leads to better L2 acquisition.

    B. Abandoning L1 leads to faster acquisition in L2.

    C. Home reading in L2 leads to faster language acquisition in L2.

    D. Reading proficiency in L1 should come before starting L2.

Think Like a Test Maker

52. Which of the following is most important when applying Sheltered Instruction Observation Protocol (SIOP) with ELLs in a fifth-grade class?

    A. Using explicit instruction using English dictionaries

    B. Requiring students to speak English while working in groups

    C. Providing students with opportunities to read and write in their first language

    D. Intermingling content knowledge with language acquisition instruction

53. A fourth-grade teacher wants to support the ELLs in the classroom. The teacher wants to use the language experience approach. Which of the following would fit this model?

    A. Using primarily speaking activities with students

    B. Using reading and writing activities with students

    C. Applying all four language skills—listening, speaking, reading and writing—into lessons

    D. Applying phonics, phonemic awareness, and morphology into classroom instruction

54. A fifth-grade class is completing a spelling test. In the class are several ELLs in the beginning stages of language acquisition. Which of the following would be most appropriate accommodation for students during the spelling test? Choose TWO.

    A. Provide students with the spelling words with the vowels missing and have them fill in the missing parts of the words.

    B. Allow the students to do another activity rather than participating in the spelling test since they do not have a command of the language yet.

    C. Partner the ELLs with a student translator to translate the spelling words from English into the home language.

    D. Have the students spell the words phonetically and provide explicit phonics instruction using the words after the spelling test is over.

55. In a seventh-grade English class, the teacher notices ELLs are struggling to comprehend the passage. Which of the following can the teacher do to support the ELLs?

    A. Provide students with a dictionary to look up confusing words.

    B. Develop students' background knowledge by talking about concepts in the reading first.

    C. Have the students write notes as they read and use the notes later during discussion.

    D. Allow the students to read another text in their first language.

56. According to the Sheltered Instruction Observation Protocol (SIOP), which of the following would be appropriate instructional techniques? Choose THREE.

    A. Slowing down to annunciate words clearly

    B. Using wait time to allow students to think about their responses

    C. Using spelling tests frequently to assess phonics

    D. Paraphrasing in English ELL's responses to questions

    E. Providing notes in English for ELLs during instruction

57. Which of the following would be most effective for ELLs in developing reading comprehension in L2 of informational text?

A. Providing students with a translated version of the text

B. Providing and using a graphic organizer before, during, and after reading

C. Allowing ELLs to work together during the reading and translate for each other

D. Providing ELLs with dictionaries to look up complex words int the text

58. Which of the following would help ELLs with visualization of academic vocabulary?

A. Word web

B. Partner reads

C. Dictionary

D. Textbook

59. An ELL is also in special education for a learning disability. Which of the following should the content area teachers focus on for this student?

A. Providing the student with a paraprofessional

B. Calling the parents frequently with updates

C. Requiring the student to do half of what is required of the other students

D. Placing the student in the least restrictive environment

60. This activity is when students fill in the blanks of a reading passage and requires the student to use comprehension.

A. Think-pair-share

B. Literature circle

C. Cloze reading

D. Venn Diagram

61. Several content area teachers are receiving professional development on cultural awareness because they will be teaching students who are ELLs. Which of the following would be a necessary part of the training?

A. ELLs need at least one year to assimilate into the new culture.

B. Teachers should communicate regularly with parents about their children.

C. Students should engage in speaking English as much as possible.

D. Culture and language are interrelated, and children learn language through their societies.

62. In a professional learning community (PLC), a high school English teacher is leading a session on differentiation for ELLs. Which of the following paradigms would be most effective as a focus of this session?

A. Using ELLs' native language as a basis for instruction in the second language.

B. Ensuring ELLs stay in an ESL or ESOL program for at least three years.

C. Encouraging students to use English only when in an academic setting.

D. Using other students as buddies to translate for ELLs to encourage collaboration.

63. When a teacher offers support and encouragement to an ELL who is struggling to read a short piece of text allowed, the teacher is:

    A. Encouraging automaticity

    B. Lowering the affective filter

    C. Differentiating instruction

    D. Using negative reinforcement

64. Which of the following would be considered being culturally responsive in the classroom?

    A. Allowing students to work in groups with peers of similar cultures

    B. Encouraging students to read aloud in class to increase their automatic reading

    C. Using supplemental text that highlights different cultures

    D. Providing students with a paraprofessional to translate when needed

65. A teacher overhears one student say to another, "You should speak English because we are in America and that is the proper way of speaking." What should the teacher do in this situation? Choose TWO.

    A. Scold the student for not being culturally responsive.

    B. Assign the student reading on how to be culturally responsive.

    C. Show students how to avoid being ethnocentric by introducing them to many different cultures.

    D. Show students a video on how implicit bias negatively affects society.

    E. Have students work in groups to roleplay culturally responsive actions based on a set of predetermined principles.

66. A teacher wants to show ELLs how interactions take place at a bank. The teacher posts a series of communication on the board:

    Teller: *"Good morning"*

    Customer: *"Good morning."*

    Teller: *"How can I help you?"*

    Customer: *"I would like to make a deposit."*

    Teller: *"It would be my pleasure to do that for you."*

    Customer: *"Thank you so much."*

    This is an example of:

    A. Notional function

    B. Language experience

    C. Total Physical Response

    D. Language fluency

67. The principal of a school with a high ELL population wants to increase parent involvement in the parent teacher organization (PTO). Over the last few years, parent participation of ELLs has declined. What can the principal and teachers do to help encourage parents of ELLs to come to PTO meetings?

A. Offer culturally diverse foods to be served at the meeting so parents get to know the different cultures at the school.

B. Provide parents with translators so they can effectively communicate their concerns at the meetings.

C. Send home information in a parent newsletter inviting parents to attend the upcoming PTO meetings.

D. Design an ad in the local newspaper letting the community know about the PTO meetings and encourage participation.

68. Which of the following is the most effective and most culturally responsive way to teach ELLs?

A. Encourage ELLs to abandon their first language and focus on the second language as much as possible.

B. Use a two-way immersion program that integrates the first language with the second language.

C. Encourage students to assimilate into their new culture so they fit in more quickly with their peers.

D. Use English only practices so students are completely immersed in the second language for quicker acquisition.

69. A teacher wants to be sure parents receive important information about an upcoming science lab. Which of the following would be the most appropriate way to ensure parents receive this information?

A. Send students home with information in the students' native languages.

B. Post about the lab on the school's website where parents can access the information.

C. Send home a detailed email with instructions about the lab.

D. Call each parent to ensure that every parent gets the information about the lab.

70. Which of the following is concerned with how people with different social identities, such as race, ethnicity, and class, speak and how their language and culture is interrelated?

A. Cultural appropriation

B. Cultural competence

C. Social justice

D. Sociolinguistics

71. A content area teacher notices that some ELLs are not motivated to do the class assignments and are not interested in participating in discussion or collaborative work. What can the teacher do to motivate these students to participate?

A. Determine the students' interest and elements of culture and incorporate that into lessons and activities.

B. Reward the students with homework passes when they participate in classroom activities and assignments.

C. Call home to speak with the parents and come up with a plan together to get the students more involved in activities.

D. Allow the students to work together in collaborative groups so they have familiarity with others and are motivated to participate.

Think Like a Test Maker

72. An ELL is displaying attributes of a learning disability. The teacher wants to intervene and help the student. Which of the following is the best approach to take first?

    A. Have the student tested for a learning disability and discuss the findings with the parents.

    B. Call the parents and ask for permission to test the student for a disability.

    C. Use a variety of multi-tiered systems of supports to scaffold for the student.

    D. Place the student in the least restrictive environment and ask for an IEP.

73. Which of the following could a teacher emphasize that would lead ELLs to participate in collaborative discussion about literature?

    A. Teachers are experts in their field and should not be questioned.

    B. Working independently is the best way to show mastery of standards.

    C. Working with others to analyze topics and express oneself are important academic skills.

    D. Required classroom activities that are graded are the best way to show mastery.

74. Jose is a seventh-grade student who has been in the United States for four years. He now speaks English fluently and dresses like his peers. He does not like to speak Spanish and avoids anything having to do with his culture. What is Jose displaying?

    A. To do better in school, Jose has used accommodations.

    B. To fit into American society, Jose has assimilated.

    C. To fit in with American society, Jose uses bilingualism.

    D. To do better in school, Jose has engaged in pluralism.

75. Two-way immersion has positive results because it promotes:

    A. English acquisition

    B. Assimilation

    C. Bilingualism

    D. Enculturation

76. An ESL teacher has several students who are speaking and writing in English. Which of the following model should be the goal for these students?

    A. Self-contained model

    B. Pull-put method

    C. Push-in method

    D. Inclusion model

77. Which of the following is the best way to design and implement instruction for a variety of ELLs who are from different countries and who speak different languages?

    A. Use English immersion so students become fluent quickly.

    B. Differentiate instruction to the specific needs of each student.

    C. Use group work often so students get to know each other.

    D. Have frequent parent conferences to communicate expectations.

78. Which of the following modifications can be applied to all students in the classroom?

    A. Tier I modifications

    B. Tier II modifications

    C. Tier III modifications

    D. Tier IV modifications

79. Which of the following is the most culturally responsive practice teachers can use in the classroom?

    A. Set clear goals for students and work with students to meet those goals.

    B. Use whole-group instruction that promotes communication skills and language acquisition.

    C. Provide students with pictures and supports during activities and exams.

    D. Offer students safe spaces and frequent opportunities to practice what they have learned.

80. Which of the following would ELLs with limited L2 benefit most from?

    A. Pictures to accompany reading and speaking activities

    B. A partner to translate for the student

    C. Frequent parent teacher conferences to communicate progress

    D. Lots of exposure to English texts

81. Which of the following assessments would be the most effective in monitoring language acquisition in ELLs?

    A. Summative assessment

    B. Screening assessment

    C. Norm-referenced assessment

    D. Formative assessment

82. WIDA delivers an assessment called ACCESS that measures:

    A. Listening, speaking, reading, and writing

    B. Language arts, math, physical education, art

    C. Language acquisition, bilingualism, and acculturation

    D. Reading knowledge and mathematical thinking

83. At the end of the year, ELLs are required to participate in which of the following standards-based assessments?

    A. Formative assessment

    B. Criterion-referenced assessment

    C. Norm-referenced assessment

    D. Screening process

84. This is an assessment used to place ELLs within four days of entering school.

    A. Formative assessment

    B. Summative assessment

    C. Universal screening

    D. Diagnostic assessment

85. An ELL has been placed in a math teacher's class. The teacher knows that the student is in his first year of second language acquisition based on initial test results. Which of the following assessments would be most effective in differentiating instruction based on the student's needs?

    A. Summative

    B. Portfolio

    C. Criterion-referenced

    D. Diagnostic

86. An ESL teacher wants to ensure that her classroom assessments are testing what they are intended to assess. She wants to assess math and is worried that the word problems may be an assessment of reading rather than math. What is the teacher considering?

    A. Validity

    B. Reliability

    C. Norm reference

    D. Criteria

87. Which of the following is the most effective use of a formative assessment? Choose TWO.

    A. To rank students based on ability

    B. To choose appropriate goals for students

    C. To group students for interventions

    D. To make instructional decisions

    E. To administer semester grades

88. A teacher is careful not to include items on her teacher-made exams that put certain groups of students at a disadvantage over others. The teacher is considering test:

    A. Reliability

    B. Validity

    C. Bias

    D. Consistency

89. An English teacher has several ELLs who are at the beginning stages of language acquisition. They are working on their speaking and listening skills. The teacher wants to test them for listening comprehension. Which of the following alternative assessments would be most appropriate if she wanted to test their listening comprehension and story sequence?

    A. Portfolio assessment

    B. Summative assessment

    C. Oral assessment

    D. Group assessment

90. These assessments have two main purposes: to identify ELLs who are eligible for services and to track and monitor English acquisition progress.

    A. Summative assessments

    B. English language proficiency assessments

    C. Portfolio assessments

    D. Formative assessments

91. An ESL teacher is working with intermediate ELLs on a one-paragraph essay. The teacher wants students to have a clear introductory sentence, three detail sentences, and a concluding sentence. Which of the following tools would be most helpful to communicate expectations so students know exactly what is expected of them for this task?

    A. Give students a rubric for the assignment before they begin and allow them to use the rubric as they write, ensuring they meet expectations along the way.

    B. Give students the instructions for the assignment printed out on a piece of paper with steps to follow in English and their home language.

    C. Have students pair up and discuss the assignment with a partner before beginning so each student understands the instructions.

    D. Post the instructions for the assignment on the board and remind students of the steps as they are writing.

92. Which of the following would be considered an alternative assessment for measuring an ELL's writing progress over the semester?

    A. Formative assessment

    B. Summative assessment

    C. Portfolio assessment

    D. Criterion-referenced assessment

93. A student who scores at a level 5 on the WIDA ACCESS would most likely:

    A. Need extensive ELL supports

    B. Need some ELL supports

    C. Need to be retested

    D. Need little ELL supports

Think Like a Test Maker

94. Which of the following is the most common accommodation for ELLs during state testing?

    A. Extended time

    B. Alternative environment

    C. Translation services

    D. Exemptions

95. Many states' board of education agencies determine whether or not to give accommodations to ELLs for state testing based on which of the following?

    A. Amount of English the student speaks at home

    B. Time the student has been in the United States in English-speaking schools

    C. Number of state reading tests the student has already taken in the United States

    D. Time student spends in ESOL or ESL classrooms vs mainstream classrooms

96. A student is assessed on the WIDA ACCESS framework. The student is at the bridging stage. This means the students is:

    A. Just beginning to learn English

    B. Uses some social and academic English with visual supports

    C. Uses social and academic English without visual supports

    D. Uses social and academic English on grade level

97. This is the degree to which scores from a particular test are consistent from one use of the test to the next.

    A. Validity

    B. Reliability

    C. Accountability

    D. Bias

98. An ESOL teacher is determining if a program she will implement at the beginning of the semester will be effective. How can she measure these outcomes?

    A. Use a summative at the beginning of the semester, formatively assess and progress monitor throughout the semester, and use a diagnostic at the end to measure outcomes.

    B. Use an oral assessment at the beginning of the semester, have student write essays during lessons, and use a norm-referenced at the end to measure success.

    C. Use a pretest at the beginning of the semester, formatively assess and progress monitor throughout the semester, and use a summative at the end to measure outcomes.

    D. Use formal assessments before, during, and after using the program and measure outcomes based on a rubric.

99. Which of the following would not be considered an alternative assessment?

    A. State-standardized test

    B. Portfolio

    C. Essay

    D. Oral assessment

100. Which of the following would be considered an objective assessment?

    A. Presentation

    B. Portfolio

    C. Multiple choice

    D. Survey

101. Which of the following court cases/policies was pivotal in determining that students must receive instruction from properly certified, licensed teachers?

    A. No Child Left Behind

    B. Plyer vs. Doe

    C. Lau vs. Nichols

    D. Every Student Succeeds Act (ESSA)

102. Which of the following is a part of intrinsic motivation?

    A. Rewards

    B. Code switching

    C. Cooperative work

    D. Autonomy

103. An ELL student is also in special education classes. Which of the following is required under IDEA for this student?

    A. Access to the general curriculum whenever possible.

    B. Supplemental materials

    C. Extra time on assessments

    D. A paraprofessional to translate and to help with behavior

104. Why is it more difficult to identify students who are ELL and who also may be gifted and talented (GT)?

    A. Teachers do not have access to measure that can help determine students' GT status.

    B. Traditional assessments for identifying GT students do not always measure ELLs properly.

    C. Most ELLs do not want to be identified as GT until they master the second language.

    D. ELLs cannot be classified at GT until they test out of ESL or ESOL classes.

Think Like a Test Maker

105. A teacher is working with ELLs who are also in a self-contained special education classroom. She will be starting a functional curriculum with these students. What would make the teacher determine that a functional curriculum is necessary?

A. The students' academic and linguistic needs are not being met in the general education classes.

B. The students are meeting proficiency in the general education classes.

C. The students' behavior plans cannot be met in the general education classes.

D. The students need paraprofessionals and translators to complete classwork.

106. A student who is ELL and wheelchair-bound is in a content area science classroom. The students will be participating in a lab. Where should the teacher place the student?

A. In the back of the classroom near the exit

B. In the front of the room near the teacher

C. In the least restrictive environment

D. With other ELLs especially for group work

107. A teacher notices that an ELL in class may be gifted. However, the student did not achieve on the traditional gifted exam. What might the teacher observe the student doing that would indicate the student is gifted but not displaying these attributes in a traditional way? Choose TWO.

A. Read above grade level in the first language

B. Problem solving in imaginative ways

C. Reading faster than the other students

D. Turning in math homework before the deadline

E. Asking to work individually rather than in groups

108. Which of the following would be considered qualitative ways to measure an ELL's abilities regarding gifted and talented (GT)?

A. Reading proficiency tests

B. Norm-referenced tests

C. State reading tests

D. Performance-based evaluations

109. This comes from Krashen's Comprehensible Input Hypothesis and is an approach to teaching ELLs which integrates language and content instruction. The goals of this approach are to provide access to general, mainstream content instruction, and promote English language proficiency.

A. Total Physical Response

B. Cognitive Academic Language Learning Approach (CALLA)

C. Sheltered Instruction Observation Protocol (SIOP)

D. Special Education Programs

110. All ELLs in the United States, whether documented or not, are entitled to this under the Consent Decree.

    A. Free school lunches

    B. After-school tutoring in English

    C. At least four yearly parent-teacher conferences

    D. Comprehensible instruction

111. According to this law, no person in the United States shall, on the ground of race, or national origin, be excluded from participation in, be denied the benefits of, or otherwise be subjected to discrimination under any problem or activity receiving federal financial assistance from the Department of Health, Education, and Welfare.

    A. The Civil Rights Act

    B. No Child Left Behind

    C. The Consent Decree

    D. Every Student Succeeds Act (ESSA)

112. This law focused on standards-based instruction and holding schools and teachers accountable for student achievement.

    A. The Consent Decree

    B. The Civil Rights Act of 1964

    C. No Child Left Behind (NCLB)

    D. Every Student Succeeds Act (ESSA)

113. Which of the following would be considered an extrinsic reward?

    A. Free homework passes they can use for the next assignment

    B. The satisfaction of knowing they did a good job

    C. Understanding the information in the homework and doing well on the test

    D. Allowing students to choose books based on interest

114. Which of the following is essential for students who are ELL and in special education classes?

    A. Extra time on assessments and assignments

    B. Individualized education programs (IEPs) that are culturally and linguistically relevant

    C. Behavior plans that include ways students can control outbursts

    D. Rewards for positive behavior

115. When teachers are not trained properly in the difference between language barriers and special needs, what is the consequence?

    A. An underrepresentation of ELLs in ESOL classes

    B. An overrepresentation of ELLs in special education classes

    C. Too much emphasis on multi-tiered system of supports

    D. Miscommunication with parents and staff

116. Which of the following are positive academic outcomes of two-way immersion?

   A. Time on task in the home language

   B. Additive bilingualism

   C. Early ESL exit exams

   D. Scripted reading and math programs

117. Fifteen, tenth-grade ELLs who have special needs are in a life skills class all day with the same teacher. What type of model is this?

   A. Total Physical Response

   B. Cognitive Academic Language Learning Approach (CALLA)

   C. Sheltered Instruction Observation Protocol (SIOP)

   D. Self-contained setting

118. Which of the following would be an example of a Total Physical Response (TPR)?

   A. Students write an essay and then workshop that essay in groups.

   B. The teacher gives explicit instruction before beginning an activity.

   C. The teacher models an action, and the students mimic that action.

   D. The students work individually on their assignments.

119. An ELL is facing suspension for an incident that happened during school. Which of the following must the school provide for this due process hearing?

   A. An interpreter who is fluent in the student's home language.

   B. An interpreter who has knowledge in both languages of any specialized terms or concepts to be used in the communication

   C. An ESOL teacher who knows the student and who can explain the process for the student and parents.

   D. A suspension guide and options for ESOL services outside of the school.

120. A teacher has multi-level students who are also ELL. Which of the following would be the best approach?

   A. Use average test results to group students.

   B. Use collaborative learning so students don't get bored.

   C. Tailor activities to individual language needs.

   D. Administer the same tests to all students for reliability.

This page intentionally left blank.

Practice Test 2 Answer Explanations

Number	Category	Answer	Explanation
1	Standards-Based Instruction	B	WIDA is a consortium of states dedicated to the design and implementation of high standards and equitable educational opportunities for English language learners. Therefore, answer B is the best answer.
2	Standards-Based Instruction	D	When students practice learner autonomy, they take charge of their learning and are invested in their outcomes. Roleplay is an effective practice, but it does not need to be practiced daily, and it is not a better answer than answer D. Grouping student homogeneously (based on level) is not best practiced daily. While it is necessary to group students and prescribe interventions, students should be in other groups with other students most of the time. At-home practices are used in education, but they are usually not the correct answer. The question is asking for daily practices, making answer D the best answer.
3	Standards-Based Instruction	A	Students who are in the early production are still learning the basics of the language. Therefore, graphic representations are best in this situation. All the other answer choices are too advanced or not as effective for students in early production. Caution: Multiple-choice test is a bad word on this exam. Avoid answer choices containing multiple-choice tests.
4	Standards-Based Instruction	C	When teachers consider students' learning preferences, they understand students may prefer to learn in a kinesthetic, auditory, or visual manner. Some students prefer working individually while others prefer cooperative learning. When teachers consider this when planning instruction, they are providing a student-centered learning environment.
5	Standards-Based Instruction	A	All the answer choices are good practices. However, the question is asking for the most effective. At the beginning of every lesson, teacher should communicate the objectives for the lesson. In addition, objectives should be measurable so the teacher can determine if the students did, in fact, learn what the lesson intended them to learn. In addition, the term *measure objectives* is on the good words list.
6	Standards-Based Instruction	B	The most important thing the teacher can do when planning instruction is to consult the state-adopted standards. That Is the first thing that should happen. Everything else comes after the standards.

Number	Category	Answer	Explanation
7	Standards-Based Instruction	C	Teaching dialect explains that even inside languages there are variations to consider when listening to someone speak. Register is the formality of language. Language acquisition is the process of learning a new language. Finally, assimilation is when students abandon their first language and customs for the new language and customs.
8	Standards-Based Instruction	D	Answer D keeps the standard high but provides support (scaffolds). This is very important when differentiating instruction for ELLs. Never lower the standards, which is what answers A-C are doing.
9	Standards-Based Instruction	B	Self-assessments are effective for helping students self-reflect and understand their stages of learning.
10	Standards-Based Instruction	A	The only activities specific to critical thinking and metacognition listed in the answer choices are in answer A: predicting and questioning. Predicting and questioning techniques are the only critically thinking activities that require the student to use higher-order thinking and activate metacognition. In addition, answer A references during reading, which is part of metacognition. Students are thinking about which processes in the brain to use to figure out text while reading.
11	Standards-Based Instruction	C	Kinesthetic learners need to move their bodies while learning, making the activity in answer C the best answer.
12	Standards-Based Instruction	C & D	Productive skills are speaking and writing skills. Receptive skills are reading and listening. The standard outlines both receptive and productive skills. C and D do not ensure the use of both receptive and productive skills for all students simultaneously, making them the correct answers to the question.
13	Standards-Based Instruction	A	Answer choice A has all the good words in it: standards and culturally responsive. Answer B is a good strategy, but not most important. Answers C and D outline ineffective practices and should be avoided.
14	Standards-Based Instruction	B & D	Answers B and D are both effective in activating background knowledge before students engage with these complex concepts.
15	Standards-Based Instruction	C	The most important thing to consider when drafting objectives is how will you measure the objective to determine if the student met the objective and whether or not the objective is culturally relevant to ELLs and all students.

Number	Category	Answer	Explanation
16	Standards-Based Instruction	B & C	Online reading programs are beneficial because they adjust and differentiate based on the students' responses to comprehension questions, which makes differentiation easy. Also, computers allow for teachers to collect important data on student reading levels and then make instructional decisions. None of the other answer choices are as beneficial as answers B and C.
17	Standards-Based Instruction	A	In answer choice A, the student is using informal language with another student, which is register.
18	Standards-Based Instruction	A	When a student has listening comprehension, the student can understand a story that is being read aloud. Answer A is the only answer choice that supports this.
19	Standards-Based Instruction	B	Limiting a student's exposure to any words is limiting a student's ability to develop. Keep academic standards high and scaffold when needed. All of the answers, except for answer B, are beneficial to ELLs.
20	Standards-Based Instruction	C	Answer C is the most effective. Allowing students to think critically in their first language is essential in developing critical thinking in the second language.
21	Foundation of Linguistics	D	According to Universal Language Principles, language is rule-governed (grammar), language is systematic (phonics), and language is arbitrary (sounds are just sounds and do not carry meaning).
22	Foundation of Linguistics	B	In most cases, you stress the third from the last syllable in words that end in *al*.
23	Foundation of Linguistics	C	In English, the b is voiced when it is in the beginning of the word, but voiceless when it is at the end of the word. Therefore, if the teacher is using the words back and jab, the best answer is C. The words are only one syllable each, so syllabication and intonation (stress patterns) are not correct. Dialect has to do with different words used in different parts of the country, which is also not correct.
24	Foundation of Linguistics	A	In English, when verbs end in -ed, the /d/ sound is **not** voiced, and it sounds like a -t. Say the words *walked, talked, shopped,* and *locked* and put your finger on your throat. You can see that the -ed at the end of the words are unvoiced, yet we pronounce the -ed like a -t. This is another reason why English is challenging to learn.
25	Foundation of Linguistics	B	**Modal verbs** express possibility or necessity. The words *can, could, may, might, must, ought to, shall, should, will, would* and *need* are modal verbs. In this case, couldn't is a modal verb. It shows importance. While *possibly* is an adverb, that is not the focus on the lesson.

Number	Category	Answer	Explanation
26	Foundation of Linguistics	A	The student incorrectly uses the pronoun *which* and should have used the pronoun who. The words *which* and *who* are relative pronouns.
27	Foundation of Linguistics	B	Phonetics is the study of speech and sounds. It is directly related to phonics, which is what answer B outlines.
28	Foundation of Linguistics	B	The sentence contains several fragments, which indicates that the student needs assistance in sentence structure. The student uses correct word choice, spelling and order. The mistakes come from sentence structure.
29	Foundation of Linguistics	D	The students are spelling phonetically or using their phonemic awareness—or understanding sounds in word—to spell. This is sometimes referred to as inventive spelling. It is an important stage of writing because it is the beginning stages of understanding the English language.
30	Foundation of Linguistics	B	Transitions help to connect sentences and give the writing flow and variance. Syntax is grammar. Semantics is meaning. Spelling is phonics.
31	Foundation of Linguistics	D	Writing is best when it is revisited again and again and revised. Many authors will say that the writing process never ends. There are always ways to make writing better. Therefore, teachers should instill in all students, not just students who are ELLs, that writing is reciprocal and requires lots of revisions.
32	Foundation of Linguistics	B	Answer B contains the error because there are two independent clauses in the sentence separated by only the coordinating conjunction. When joining two independent clauses, a comma + a coordinating conjunction (FANBOYS) is necessary. All of the other sentences are correct.
33	Foundation of Linguistics	C	A. Phonemic awareness – smallest units of sounds in words. B. Phonics – letter-sound correspondence C. Morphology – smallest units of meaning in words (compound words, prefixes, suffixes, and roots) D. Alphabetic principle - the idea that letters and letter patterns represent the sounds of spoken language.
34	Foundation of Linguistics	C	Probably one of the most confusing parts of English is the use of the schwa (ə) sound. It is sometimes referred to as the reduced vowel sound in a word. It can be confusing to ELLs who are working on proper pronunciation of words. However, in English, we often do not fully pronounce vowel sounds in words, such as the *e* sound in *problem*.

Number	Category	Answer	Explanation
35	Foundation of Linguistics	D	In English, some sounds require the use of our voice while others do not. To test this, you can put your fingers gently on your voice box while saying the following sounds. For voiced sounds, you will feel a vibration. For voiceless sounds you will not feel a vibration.
36	Foundation of Linguistics	A	A free morpheme can stand alone because they mean something in and of themselves. For example, in the word **closely**, the morpheme **close** is a free morpheme. It can stand alone. None of the other words can be broken apart and stand on their own. They all need the entire word to make sense.
37	Foundation of Linguistics	A	Trigraphs are three-letter (tri-) combinations that create one phoneme. The first set of words contain *tch, ght, ght,* which are all trigraphs.
38	Foundation of Linguistics	B	A compound sentence contains two independent clauses. Ensure that there is a comma between two independent clauses in a compound sentence. The comma should be followed by a coordinating conjunction (**FANBOYS**). She waited for the bus, and she read her book.
39	Foundation of Linguistics	C	The student is using *sleeped* instead of *slept, waked* instead of *woke,* and *goed* instead of *went.* These are irregular verbs, and the student is applying general past-tense rules to them incorrectly.
40	Foundation of Linguistics	D	Phonics is about letter-sound relationships, which is identified in answer D.
41	Foundations of Language Acquisition	C	Second-language acquisition occurs most easily with meaningful interaction in social settings. In addition, the word *meaningful* is a good word in the answer choices.
42	Foundations of Language Acquisition	D	In most states, students who exit an ESL or ESOL program are monitored for two years. This eliminates answer A. Answer B is incorrect because once a student is out of the program, he or she does not stay in ESL or ESOL classes. Answer C is incorrect because students who are native speakers of English do not have to score proficiently on state-mandated exams to be in non-ESL or ESOL classes.
43	Foundations of Language Acquisition	D	In second language acquisition, support in L1 while learning L2 is key. Never abandon L1. Research shows that students acquire a second language most effectively when they have cognitive support in L1 while learning L2.

Number	Category	Answer	Explanation
44	Foundations of Language Acquisition	A	Comprehensible input hypothesis explains that students learn best when they take in information in a low-anxiety environment. According to Krashen (1981), language acquisition requires meaningful interaction in the target language.
45	Foundations of Language Acquisition	B	In English, the adjectives come before the nouns. For example, "I went to the pretty beach." In this case, the student is experiencing language interference because in Spanish, the adjectives come after the noun as in, "Fui a la playa bonita." Code switching is when a student incorporates words from the first language as in, "I went to the bonita beach." Language convergence is when linguistic change in which languages come to structurally resemble one another as a result of prolonged language contact and mutual interference.
46	Foundations of Language Acquisition	C	This question has to do with register—the formal vs informal nature of language depending on who the students are speaking with. The reason C is the best answer is because students are engaging in roleplay, which makes the activity relevant to the real world. Answer A is okay because it mentions register, but roleplay is the best answer here.
47	Foundations of Language Acquisition	B	Sometimes students who come from other countries have interruptions in their formal education in their first language. This can set the student back. It does not necessarily mean the student has a disability. Be careful of answer choices that automatically assign a disability to ELLs. Remember, we want to avoid disproportionately representing ELLs as needing special education when the issue is language acquisition and not a disability.
48	Foundations of Language Acquisition	C	All students should be held to high expectations. Answers A, B, and D lower the expectations for ELLs and are incorrect.
49	Foundations of Language Acquisition	B	Roleplay is usually the correct answer in situations like this. Roleplay is a relevant and real-word activity that helps students develop their conversational English, which is what Che is struggling with in this situation.
50	Foundations of Language Acquisition	C	Because the students are working on oral language, speaking centers is most appropriate.
51	Foundations of Language Acquisition	A	The most important thing to remember when teaching ELLs is that they need support in their first language to acquire a second language. They do not have to be proficient in L1 first. Many first and second graders just learning to read can become proficient in L1 and L2 simultaneously. Also, avoid answer choices where students must abandon L1 or engage in English only practices.

Number	Category	Answer	Explanation
52	Foundations of Language Acquisition	D	Sheltered instruction comes from Krashen's Comprehensible Input Hypothesis and is an approach to teaching ELLs which integrates language and content instruction. Therefore, answer D is the best answer.
53	Foundations of Language Acquisition	C	The Language Experience Approach (LEA) is a literacy development method that has been used for early reading development with ELLs. This approach combines all four language skills: listening, speaking, reading, and writing.
54	Foundations of Language Acquisition	A & D	The best accommodations are A and D because they require the students to participate and keep standards high, yet there are scaffolds built in. Providing the students with the words with the vowels missing is an accommodation where the students still have to participate in the spelling test, but they have support. Allowing ELLs to spell phonetically helps to build their phonemic awareness skills. Then the teacher can focus on phonics after that. Answer B lowers the standards for ELLs, and answer C requires other students to translate during their test, which is ineffective.
55	Foundations of Language Acquisition	B	Developing the students' background knowledge is the best answer choice. All the other answer choices either lower the standards or provide students with inappropriate supports. For example, a dictionary will do little to help a student. Taking notes while reading will also do little to help a student. Allowing the student to read a different book in the first language avoids the standard of reading the text required in class.
56	Foundations of Language Acquisition	A, B, & D	All the following align with SIOP except answers C and E. Using spelling tests frequently can be helpful but is not part of SIOP. Providing notes to ELLs is also not part of SIOP. The goals of Sheltered Instruction Observation Protocol are to provide access to general, mainstream content instruction, and promote English language proficiency. Answers A, B, and D do that.
57	Foundations of Language Acquisition	B	Graphic organizers are effective ways to help all students comprehend text and is the most effective practice listed.
58	Foundations of Language Acquisition	A	A word web is a visualization of vocabulary words. A word web is usually administered as a graphic organizer.
59	Foundations of Language Acquisition	D	Remember, in a least restrictive environment (LRE) students with disabilities should have access to general education curriculum whenever possible. Therefore, you should look for answer choices where teachers are helping students through accommodations and modifications to access that curriculum.

Number	Category	Answer	Explanation
60	Founda-tions of Language Acquisition	C	Cloze reading activities require students to fill in the blanks in a short reading passage, which tests their reading comprehension.
61	Cultural Awareness	D	One of the most important things an ESL or ESOL teacher can understand is that culture and language are interrelated. Rossi-Landi (1973) asserts children learn their language from their societies, and during the process of learning a language also learn their culture and develop their cognitive abilities.
62	Cultural Awareness	A	Answer A is the only one listed that is appropriate practice. Supporting ELLs' first languages is very important. The rest of the answer choices are not considered best practices.
63	Cultural Awareness	B	Lowering the affective filter is providing the student with support and making the student feel comfortable. When the affective filter is high, students feel unmotivated and anxious. The teacher in this situation is helping the student feel more comfortable and, therefore, lowering the affective filter.
64	Cultural Awareness	C	Only answer C is culturally responsive. Showcasing other cultures through literature is one way teachers can promote culture awareness in the classroom.
65	Cultural Awareness	C & E	Both C and E are appropriate ways the teacher can be culturally responsive in this situation. Ethnocentricity is when a person uses one's own culture as the basis of judgment of other cultures, which is what is happening in this situation. Therefore, answer C is correct. In addition, exposing students to other cultures will help them be more culturally aware and less likely to be ethnocentric and bias. Answers A, B, and D are not effective.
66	Cultural Awareness	A	The notional-functional approach in ESL or ESOL instruction is a way of designing classroom instruction and materials around *notions* or real-life situations. This includes the way people communicate Then these *notions* are further broken down into *functions* or specific ways of communication.
67	Cultural Awareness	B	Providing parents with translators to communicate meaningful topics is most important for this situation. A newsletter and newspaper are not effective modes of communication for this. Providing food is a plus. However, it is not the most appropriate here.
68	Cultural Awareness	B	Always choose bilingualism or two-way immersion programs. Never expect students to abandon their first language or culture.

Number	Category	Answer	Explanation
69	Cultural Awareness	A	The best answer is to send home the information in the students' home languages. Posting on the website or sending an email is problematic for two reasons: not everyone has access to the Internet, and sending an email and posting online does not include native languages. Calling every parent is not realistic.
70	Cultural Awareness	D	Sociolinguistics the study of language in relation to social factors. It is also focused on how culture and language are interrelated.
71	Cultural Awareness	A	Intrinsic motivation is the best answer, and answer A outlines that. Determining their interests and parts of their culture and incorporating that into lessons will motivate the ELLs to engage. This is the best answer out of the four choices.
72	Cultural Awareness	C	Before jumping in and automatically testing the student or calling the parents, it is best to apply a system of supports to see if scaffolding and using supports helps the student. If that doesn't work, then the teacher can speak to the special education coordinator for what to do next. Teachers must be careful that they do not skip steps in this process.
73	Cultural Awareness	C	Answer C is best because it mentions working with others, which is part of the question. It also includes analytical thinking, which is higher-order thinking and essential in improving academic skills.
74	Cultural Awareness	B	Assimilation is when two cultures compete, and the minority culture is abandoned. Jose has abandoned his first language and culture to fit into American society.
75	Cultural Awareness	C	Bilingualism is the goal. We do not want students to assimilate and abandon their culture. Bilingualism preserves students' cultures and L1.
76	Cultural Awareness	D	Inclusion should always be the goal. Teachers must work to get students into mainstream classrooms with their peers.
77	Cultural Awareness	B	The most culturally responsive thing to do in this situation is differentiate based on students' specific needs.
78	Cultural Awareness	A	Tier I modifications are differentiated instructional methods *all* students get in the form of academic and behavior/social-emotional supports. Tier I is basic and general implementation of the core curriculum that is aligned to the state standards.
79	Cultural Awareness	D	Answer D is the most culturally responsive because it provides students with a safe space to speak and practice the new language. Be careful not to choose answer A because setting goals for students is not culturally responsive. Students should set their own goals. Answers B and C are not as culturally responsive as answer D.

Number	Category	Answer	Explanation
80	Cultural Awareness	A	A student with limited English proficiency would benefit most from pictures to accompany text. Pictures are a helpful aid for those in the early production stage of language acquisition.
81	Assessment	D	A formative assessment is used to monitor progress. It is an ongoing, informal assessment and the best answer for this situation.
82	Assessment	A	WIDA ACCESS assesses the four language domains of listening, speaking, reading, and writing.
83	Assessment	B	Criterion-referenced assessments measures student performance against a fixed set of predetermined criteria or learning standards.
84	Assessment	C	Screening assessments are used to place students in appropriate classes where they can receive appropriate interventions and instruction.
85	Assessment	D	A diagnostic assessment would help the teacher identify specific skills the student needs help with. Then the teacher can prescribe interventions and differentiate instruction.
86	Assessment	A	Validity is the degree to which a test score can be interpreted and used for its intended purpose.
87	Assessment	C & D	Formative assessments are used to make instructional decisions. They are ongoing and used to help differentiate instruction. Answers C and D outline the use of a formative assessment.
88	Assessment	C	Test bias is test design that systematically disadvantages certain groups of students over others, such as students of color, students from lower-income backgrounds, students who are not proficient in the English language, or students who are not fluent in certain cultural customs and traditions.
89	Assessment	C	An oral assessment is an alternative assessment teachers can use to test students' speaking and listening skills. Oral assessments are especially helpful in assessing students who are not yet proficient in writing English.
90	Assessment	B	English language proficiency (ELP) assessments have two main purposes: to identify ELLs and to track proficiency.
91	Assessment	A	For assignments like writing and projects, it is best to use a rubric students can reference while they are completing the assignment, so they understand expectations. The question references that these students are intermediate ELLs; therefore, giving them instructions in their home language is not necessary. And that choice is not better than a rubric. The other answer choices are less effective than answer A.

Think Like a Test Maker

Number	Category	Answer	Explanation
92	Assessment	C	A portfolio is an alternative assessment that contains artifacts (in this case writing examples) of student work collected over a specific period of time.
93	Assessment	D	A student who scores a level 5 on the WIDA ACCESS will most likely test out of ESOL or ESL by most states' standards. The states that use ACCESS usually set 5 as the level where the student no longer receives ELL supports and is put into full-time mainstream classes.
94	Assessment	A	Extended time is the most common accommodation for ELLs taking state exams. Many states will give time and a half or even as much time needed for students who are designated ELL.
95	Assessment	B	One of the measures states use to determine if a student qualifies for accommodations such as extra time is how long the student has been in the United States or in English-speaking schools.
96	Assessment	D	According to WIDA bridging is a level 5. In many states this is the level at which students score to test out of ESL or ESOL programs.
97	Assessment	B	Reliability is the degree to which the results of an assessment are consistent among and between administrations. That's why on state tests, the environment is controlled, and everyone does the same thing. It contributes to reliability.
98	Assessment	C	A preassessment will give the teacher a baseline to measure where students are before starting the program. The formative assessments will help the teacher progress monitor and make decisions. Finally, the summative is a post-test that will measure outcomes. This is the most effective series of assessments to use.
99	Assessment	A	Alternative assessments are authentic, comprehensive, and performance based. Standardized tests are not alternative assessments.
100	Assessment	C	Multiple-choice assessments have definitive answers. Therefore, they are objective. The other assessments can be open to a teacher's interpretation and are subjective.
101	Advocating for ELLs	C	This is a landmark case pertaining to language minority education. The San Francisco school system failed to provide English language instruction to 1,800 limited-English proficient Chinese students. The Court of Appeals ruled that students must receive instruction from properly certified, licensed teachers.
102	Advocating for ELLs	D	Autonomy has to do with students' independence and self-governance. Allowing students to decide how and what they learn helps to increase autonomy and increase motivation.

Number	Category	Answer	Explanation
103	Advocating for ELLs	A	Under IDEA, students must have access to the general curriculum and be educated with their peers as much as possible. Answers B, C, and D all may be options for a special needs student; however, that depends on the student's IEP. Only answer A is a guarantee under IDEA.
104	Advocating for ELLs	B	Traditional measures for GT can be inequitable for ELLs, whose language output and cultural orientation may mask their giftedness.
105	Advocating for ELLs	A	When the needs of an ELL, special education student are not met in the general education classes, supplementary or functional curriculum may be necessary. However, it is important to try to keep students in general education as much as possible.
106	Advocating for ELLs	C	Remember, in a least restrictive environment (LRE), students with disabilities have access to general education curriculum whenever possible. This student is in a wheelchair and is ELL. However, the student should receive the same education as his or her peers.
107	Advocating for ELLs	A & B	Both answers A and B are alternative ways ELLs may display gifted and talented attributes that may not show up on traditional exams.
108	Advocating for ELLs	D	Answer D is the only qualitative assessment. Answers A, B, and C are quantitative.
109	Advocating for ELLs	C	SIOP is a research-based instructional model that is effective in developing the academic skills of ELLs and is grounded in Krashen's input hypothesis.
110	Advocating for ELLs	D	The Consent Decree addresses civil and academic rights of ELLs and requires instruction be delivered in a comprehensible manner so ELLs can fully participate.
111	Advocating for ELLs	A	Title VI of the Civil Rights Act (1964) states no person in the United States shall, on the ground of race, or national origin, be excluded from participation in, be denied the benefits of, or otherwise be subjected to discrimination under any problem or activity receiving federal financial assistance from the Department of Health, Education, and Welfare.
112	Advocating for ELLs	C	No Child Left Behind (NCLB) was the main law for K–12 general education in the United States from 2002–2015 was NCLB.
113	Advocating for ELLs	A	Extrinsic motivation refers to behavior that is driven by external rewards. A homework pass is an extrinsic reward.
114	Advocating for ELLs	B	IEPs should be tailored to students who also need language supports.

Number	Category	Answer	Explanation
115	Advocating for ELLs	B	When teachers cannot decipher between language barriers and special needs, the consequence is an overrepresentation of students in special education classes who should not be there. That is why it is essential that teachers and leadership are trained in these areas.
116	Advocating for ELLs	B	Two-way immersion programs are bilingual programs. Bi means two, and bilingual programs, according to research, are the most effective ways to teach ELLs.
117	Advocating for ELLs	D	When students have severe disabilities and their needs cannot be met in the general education classrooms, they will be placed in a self-contained classroom where they have the same teacher all day and work on life skills (functional curriculum).
118	Advocating for ELLs	C	Total Physical Response (TPR) uses movement to teach language and vocabulary. The only physical action listed is in answer C.
119	Advocating for ELLs	B	According to the U.S. Department of Justice, school districts should ensure that interpreters and translators have knowledge in both languages of any specialized terms or concepts to be used in the communication at issue and are trained on the role of an interpreter and translator, the ethics of interpreting and translating, and the need to maintain confidentiality
120	Advocating for ELLs	C	Tailoring activities to each student's needs is the best way to advocate for all ELLs.

This page intentionally left blank.

Writing Task

Some ESL or ESOL teacher certification exams will require you to write an open or constructed response. Whether or not your test has a writing task, I recommend you complete the sample response in this section of the book because completing this section will strengthen your critical thinking skills, which are essential for passing the test.

Here are a few *think like a test maker* tips when tackling this part of your exam:

1. Work backwards and start with the task first. Determine what is expected of you before you read the scenario or the passage.

2. Determine how many things you are required to do and make each one its own paragraph. This helps to organize your thoughts and helps to keep things organized for the person grading your essay.

3. Be sure to complete everything laid out in the task.

4. Use specific details to explain your claims, position, or ideas. Generalizations are not good enough. Use specifics from the passage to support your writing.

5. Use the good words and information from the study guide. You just went through over 150 pages of information. When writing, use the terms and practices from the book in your essay to show your content knowledge.

Sample Writing Task

A middle school ESL teacher uses several strategies for monitoring ELLs' academic language acquisition, literacy development, metacognition, and comprehension. In a formative assessment, the teacher has sixth-grade ELLs silently read a short passage from a grade-level social studies textbook. Then the teacher has them complete a written task related to the text. The following is an excerpt from the passage and one student's response.

> Early humans were hunter-gatherers. For food, humans hunted animals and gathered plants and berries. When hunter-gatherers could not find enough to eat, they moved to another location to find food. In addition to food, early humans needed shelter and depended on the natural environment for protection and shelter. Some groups lived in caves while others lived on plains. Many made shelters out of branches, plant fibers, or animal skins.
>
> Hunter-gatherers lived together in small groups called bands, each made up of several families. The size of a group was usually around 30 people. The people who lived together reflected the number of people who could live off the plants and animals in each region. Men hunted and fished, and women gathered food, such as berries and nuts from plants that grew nearby. Children also contributed to the system by gathering and helping to obtain food.

The teacher asks students to describe the main idea of this passage in their own words. Shown below is one student's written response. According to the student's WIDA ACCESS scores, the student is an expanding-level English language learner.

> People who were living a long time ago hunted and gathered for food. The mans hunted and the womans gathered. The childrens helped too. All of the people lived together in groups so they could help each other get the food. The people depended on the land for everything even shelter.

Task

- Identify and describe one area of *strength* in the student's academic language proficiency and literacy development in English (e.g., reading comprehension, application of reading comprehension skills and strategies, knowledge of general academic and content-specific vocabulary, application of writing conventions, knowledge of Standard English)

- Identify and describe one area for *improvement* in the student's academic language proficiency and literacy development in English (e.g., reading comprehension, application of reading comprehension skills and strategies, knowledge of general academic and content-specific vocabulary, application of writing conventions, knowledge of Standard English); and

- Identify and describe one instructional strategy you would use to address the area for improvement you have identified.

Think Like a Test Maker

Notice there are three main tasks for this open response represented by the bullets. It would be helpful to make a paragraph for each task. Therefore, this will be a three-paragraph essay.

Sample Essay

A major strength in this student's writing is the student's ability to summarize. The student did gather the main points of the passage. The student did not get distracted by too many details and only focused on the main points. For example, the student left out the key details of berries and fish and stuck to the main points of men hunting and women gathering. In addition, the student has a concluding sentence that drives the main idea—early humans depended on the land for everything (food and shelter). This shows strength in reading comprehension and deciphering key details from the central theme.

One weakness the student has is the use of plural irregular nouns. The students used *mans* instead of *men*, *womans* instead of *women*, and *childrens* instead of *children*. This shows a gap in understanding grammar conventions. Therefore, while the student has a grasp on complex skills like comprehension, main idea, and key details in text, the student will need some explicit instruction in irregular plural nouns.

This is a relatively easy intervention to make to help this student fix the errors in the writing. The first intervention the teacher can use is explicit instruction in irregular plural nouns. This can be done by using word lists of irregular plural nouns. Then the student can work on using these words correctly in sentences and even revise the summary the student submitted. Finally, the teacher can teach the student to use the original passage to see how the irregular words are properly used.

Score

This response would score well on a writing assessment for several reasons:

- Everything outlined in the task is addressed. The response includes a strength with specific examples and support. It also identifies a weakness with specific examples from the response. Finally, it offers a specific strategy to use to help fix the weakness.

- The essay cites specific details throughout the response. It points to exact places in the response to support assertions.

- The response uses content knowledge by using terminology and explanations in relevant to teaching ELLs writing.

Writing Task

Reference Pages

This page intentionally left blank.

Good Words List

When I make study guides, I like to focus on *good words* in the answer choices to determine correct and incorrect answers. Good words are terms and phrases taken from the test specifications that highlight best practices. If you see these words or phrases in answer choices on the exam, slow down and have a closer look. There is a good possibility these words are in the correct answer choice. I have also included a list of bad words and phrases to avoid.

Accommodations. Modifying instruction or using supports to help special education students achieve. Accommodations do NOT involve lowering the standard or delaying learning.

Action research. The process of evaluating data in the classroom to identify issues and implementing effective and quick actions to solve problems.

Assessments. Using formative and summative data to monitor progress and measure outcomes.

Authentic instruction. Providing students with meaningful, relevant, and useful learning experiences and activities.

Balanced literacy. Reading and writing instruction that uses a variety of literary genres including literary and informational texts.

Bilingual instruction. Helping students use elements of their first language to support learning in English.

Celebrate culture. Finding materials and resources to celebrate the different cultures represented in your classroom.

Collaborative learning. These are strategies that are student-centered and self-directed rather than led by the teacher. Collaboration can also be working with colleagues or stakeholders to improve, create, or produce something.

Comprehensible education. Make information and lessons understandable to students by accommodating and using ancillary materials to help with language barriers.

Critical thinking. Higher-order thinking skills that involve evaluating, analyzing, creating, and applying knowledge.

Cultural responsiveness. Instruction as a pedagogy that empowers students intellectually, socially, and emotionally by celebrating and learning about other cultures. This includes recognizing the importance of including students' cultural references in all aspects of learning and designing a productive learning environment.

Data-driven decisions. Using scores, writing samples, observations, and other types of qualitative and quantitative data to make instructional decisions.

Developmentally appropriate instruction (DAP). Choosing text, tools, and activities that are appropriate for the students' grade level.

Differentiated instruction. Providing all learners in a diverse classroom with different methods to understand instruction.

Diversity as an asset. Seeing diversity in the classroom as an opportunity to learn new things through the perspectives of others.

Evidence-based. Providing instruction using materials with the best scientific evidence available.

Graphic organizers. Visual representations of content. Especially useful for illustrating concepts like cause and effect, problem and solution, compare and contrast, etc. ELLs thrive when they have access to visuals.

High expectations for ALL learners. Holding all students to high academic standards regardless of the students' achievement level, ethnicity, language, socioeconomic status.

Horizontal alignment. Organization and coordination of standards and learning goals across content areas in the same grade level.

Inclusive. Providing students with resources and experiences that represent their culture and ethnicity.

Interdisciplinary activities. Activities that connect two or more content areas; promotes relevance and critical thinking.

Interpreters for parents. For open house, parent-teacher conferences, and due process hearings, arranging for an interpreter for parents is a good idea.

Intrinsic motivation. Answers that promote autonomy, relatedness, and competence are ways to apply intrinsic motivation. Be on the lookout for these answer choices.

Metacognition. Analysis of your own thinking.

Minimal error corrections. This is when teachers allow ELLs to make mistakes without correcting them right away. This allows the student to continue reading or talking without interruptions.

Modeling. Demonstrating the application of a skill or knowledge.

Modifications. Changes to the curriculum and learning environment to meet the needs of ELLs.

Outcomes. The results of a program, strategy, or resources implemented in the classroom.

Performance assessment. An activity assigned to students to assess their mastery of multiple learning goals aligned to standards.

Primary resource. These are materials and information in their original form like diaries, journals, songs, paintings, and autobiographies.

Prior knowledge. What students know about a topic from their previous experiences and learning.

Progress monitor. Keeping track of student or whole class learning in real time. Quantifiable measures of progress, conferring, observing, exit tickets, and student self-assessments.

Relevance, real-world, and relatable. Be sure to choose answers that promote real-world application and make learning relatable to students' lives.

Reliable. Consistent. Producing consistent results under similar conditions.

Remediation. Correcting or changing something to make it better.

Rigorous. A word used to describe curriculum that is challenging and requires students to use higher-order thinking skills.

Scaffolding. Using supports to help students achieve a standard that they would not achieve on their own.

Specific and meaningful feedback. More than just a grade at the top of a paper, effective feedback includes positive aspects and how students can apply those positive aspects to improving. In addition, feedback should contain specific things the student should do to improve.

Standards-aligned. Ensuring that curriculum and instruction is aligned to the state-adopted standards.

Student centered/learner centered. A variety of educational programs, learning experiences, instructional approaches, and academic-support strategies that address students' distinct learning needs, interests, or cultural backgrounds.

Validity. Accuracy. How accurately knowledge or skills are measured.

Vertical alignment. Organization of standards and learning goals across grade levels. Structure for which learning and understanding is built from grade level to grade level.

Visuals. ELLs need visuals to help them understand L2.

Vocabulary in-context. Always teach vocabulary in context. It helps to relate the vocabulary to the real world.

Wait time. Time between a question and when a student is called on or a response to a student's reply.

Word consciousness. Students are aware and interested in words and word meanings. Students who are word conscious also notice when and how new words are used. Word-conscious students are motivated to learn new words and to be able to use them skillfully.

Bad Words List

Bias. Inserting personal beliefs, stereotypes, and assumptions in the learning process. This can also include learning materials developed from the perspective of the dominant culture that exclude minority perspectives.

Extra homework. On this exam, students should be getting all of the instruction they need in class. In real life, we all assign homework. However, on this exam, extra homework is not the correct answer choice.

Extrinsic motivators. These are rewards of extrinsic value like pizza parties, recess time, etc. Students should be motivated by intrinsic motivators like self-confidence, sense of accomplishment, and feeling successful.

Homogenous grouping. Grouping by gender, English proficiency, or learning level is never a best practice on this exam or in your classroom. Homogenous groups should only be used in special circumstances and on a temporary basis.

Punitive solutions. Avoid answer choices that sound like punishments. For this exam, teachers are expected to be implementing positive behavior support methods, so avoid any answer choices that sound punitive.

Requesting outside help. Often, you will see an option to request a paraprofessional or an outside aid to differentiate for the teacher. That is usually not the correct answer.

Silent independent reading. When this practice is attached to a struggling reader scenario it is usually not the correct answer because if students are struggling, reading independently is not going to help them get better.

Standardized test-taking strategies. While students need to be strategic and learn how to approach their state exams, this concept is usually not the correct answer on the exam.

Bad Words List

This page intentionally left blank.

Fluency and Reading Comprehension

On many ESL or ESOL exams, fluency and reading comprehension are not explicitly addressed. However, I think it is important to share helpful fluency and reading comprehension information that will help you with this exam.

Demonstrate knowledge of key indicators of reading fluency.

Fluency is defined as the ability to read with speed, accuracy, and proper expression, and it is a necessary skill for reading comprehension. For students to understand text, they must first read through the text with fluency. They can focus on meaning rather than sounding out words.

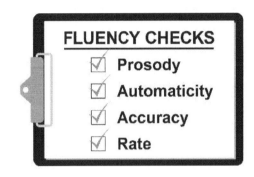

Comprehension is the essence of reading. Comprehension is when students begin to form images in their minds as they read. They are able to predict what might happen next in a story because they understand what is currently happening. Students who are in the comprehension stage of reading do not need to decode (sound out) words. They read **fluently** with **prosody**, **automaticity**, and **accuracy**.

Teachers perform **fluency checks** or **fluency reads** to measure students' reading progress. While the student reads, the teacher follows along. As the student reads, the teacher checks for **automaticity**, which is effortless, speedy word recognition. The teacher also checks the student's **accuracy** and **rate**.

- **Prosody** – comprises timing, phrasing, emphasis, and intonation that readers use to help convey aspects of meaning and to make their speech lively. Prosody includes stopping at periods, pausing at commas, reading with inflection, and reading with expression.

- **Automaticity** – is the fast, effortless word recognition that comes with repeated reading practice. When students are reading at > 95% accuracy, they have automaticity.

- **Accuracy** – is the number of words a student reads correctly. Typically, accuracy is measured by having students read aloud during a fluency read (also called a running record). The student reads, and the teacher marks any words the student miscues.

- **Rate** – is the speed at which students read words correctly. Rate is typically expressed in correct words per minute (wpm).

Demonstrate knowledge of the role of fluency at various stages of reading development.

Stages of Fluency

Like the other foundational skills discussed in this study guide, fluency has definitive stages students move through as they acquire the skill. The following are the general stages of fluency.

1. Accurate, automatic letter naming
2. Word reading
3. Reading connected text
4. Reading complex academic texts

It is important to identify and understand the interrelationship among decoding skills (phonics and word analysis), fluency, and reading comprehension.

- Fluency is the bridge between decoding and comprehension.
- Prosody is the bridge between fluency and comprehension

Be sure you understand that accuracy and automaticity is not the only part of fluency. Prosody, or reading with expression, helps students comprehend text. Speed-reading through the text without expression can hinder compression. Teachers can help students with their prosody by modeling good prosody during read-alouds.

Demonstrate knowledge of the importance of providing students with frequent opportunities to develop and extend their fluency development at different stages of reading development.

Fluency supports cognitive endurance. When students have the cognitive endurance to read through large sections of text and build meaning from that text, they are not wasting cognitive energy on decoding words. Instead, students are reading fluently, using their cognitive energy toward comprehension and critical thinking.

Fluency is important because it allows students to use cognitive energy on building comprehension of text, rather than using cognitive energy on sounding out words. All of the following strategies are effective for English language learners (ELLs) as well.

Example Problem

A teacher encourages second-grade ELL students to take a decodable passage home and read it two times each night for five nights. The primary purpose of this strategy would be to increase:

A. Comprehension

B. Phonics

C. Automaticity

D. Metacognition

Correct Answer: C

This is a repeated reading exercise. Repeated reading helps to increase automaticity and fluency.

Apply knowledge of evidence-based, explicit strategies for promoting fluency.

Fluency is important because it allows students to use cognitive energy on building comprehension of text rather than using cognitive energy on sounding out words. The following instructional methods work to develop fluency and are effective strategies to increase automaticity, accuracy, prosody, and rate.

Choral Reading - Reading aloud in unison with a whole class or group of students. Choral reading helps build students' fluency, self-confidence, and motivation. Choral reading can be done a variety of ways.

- **Unison** – The whole class reads together in unison.

- **Refrain** – One student reads the narrative part of the text; the rest of the class reads the refrain.

- **Antiphon** – The class is divided in two groups; one group reads one part, and the other group reads the other part.

Repeated Reading – Reading passages again and again, aiming to read more words correctly per minute each time. This helps to increase automaticity.

Running Records – Following along as a student reads and marking when he or she makes a mistake or miscues. At the end, the teacher counts how many words per minute (wpm) the student read correctly.

Miscue Analysis – Looking over the running record, analyzing why the student miscued and employing strategies to help the student with miscues.

Conferencing – Conferencing individually with students to go over fluency goals and strategies is very effective. Teachers and students can look over fluency data and decide how to move forward to build better fluency.

Data folders – Often, students will keep their fluency data in a data folder. It is effective to chart progress over time so students can see their growth. Data should be kept confidential and only discussed between the teacher, student, and parents.

The following question is how developing fluency might be presented on the exam.

Fluency Strategy	Definition	Example	Helps with...
Basal reading	Leveled reading books	Dick and Jane series	Automaticity
Running records	Assessing students' fluency by determining the student's rate or how many words per minute (wpm) a student reads correctly.	Following along as a student reads and marking when he or she makes a mistake or miscues. At the end, the teacher counts how many words per minute (wpm) the student read correctly.	Automaticity, accuracy, rate, prosody
Miscue analysis	Looking over the running record, analyzing why the student miscued and employing strategies to help the student with miscues.	After a fluency read, the teacher and student analyze the mistakes the student made and come up with strategies to fix those mistakes.	Accuracy
Repeated reading	Reading text that is at students' independent reading level over and over again to help with fluency.	The teacher has a student read a passage and then re-read the passage several times over the course of a week to build automaticity and reading confidence.	Automaticity, rate, accuracy, prosody
Readers' theater	A strategy for developing reading fluency. It engages students by having them read parts of a script.	Students are reading a story; each student is one of the characters in the book. Students read aloud through the text.	Prosody
Choral reading	Reading aloud in unison through a piece of text.	The teacher uses choral reading with ELL students to help them with fluency and confidence.	Accuracy, prosody
Silent sustained reading	Students read silently on their own.	The teacher dedicates 15 minutes every day to having students read their novels on their own.	Automaticity, accuracy, rate, prosody

Apply evidence-based, explicit strategies for prosody

There are several ways teachers can differentiate instruction when guiding students through fluency skills.

- **Teacher modeling** – When the teacher reads aloud, the teacher models effective fluency strategies in decoding, word analysis and recognition, and prosody. The teacher can do this by thinking aloud and demonstrating the thought process used when encountering difficult words.

- **Phrase-cued reading** – A phrase-cued text is a written passage that is divided according to natural pauses that occur in and between sentences. The pauses help students whose reading lacks prosody read with expression and with proper pacing. These types of texts also help students group words together for fluent reading.

- **Echo reading** – This involves the teacher reading aloud a text line by line or sentence by sentence modeling appropriate fluency. After reading each line, the students echo back the reading of the line with the same rate and prosody.

Quick Tip

Building students' familiarity with complex academic language structures by increasing students' background knowledge is essential in helping students increase their fluency and ultimately their comprehension. Having background knowledge or schema can positively impact fluency.

Apply evidence-based, explicit strategies for differentiation

Teachers must use a balanced literacy approach in the classroom. This means they are using both informational and literary texts. On the exam, be on the lookout for answers that outline teachers using both literary and informational text in the content area to support reading across disciplines. The following is how this might look on the exam.

Example Problem

An fourth-grade health teacher wants ELLs to read a news article about a new health study involving kids and sleep. The teacher knows the text will be complex for some students who struggle. Which of the following would be most effective to support these students?

    A. Have struggling students take home extra reading for homework.

    B. Have students use silent sustained reading in class.

    C. Use a variety of leveled text and differentiate instruction based on needs.

    D. Have the reading coach come in and teach the class.

Correct Answer: C

When it comes to content area literacy, answer C has all the good words you should look for in the answer choices—*variety of levels, differentiated instruction, based on needs*. Extra homework and silent sustained reading are usually not the best answer choices. And having the reading coach teach your class is not the most effective.

Fluency and Reading Comprehension

To differentiate instruction, the teacher must understand students' reading levels. The table below breaks down reading levels in terms of fluency. This will be discussed further in the assessment section of the student guide.

Reading Level	Accuracy	Example
Independent	≥ 95%	A student easily reads through a paragraph, exercising prosody and automaticity. The student makes only one error.
Instructional	90%	A student reads through a paragraph, mostly exercising prosody and automaticity. The student makes only six errors, but self-corrects on most of the errors.
Frustration	< 90%	The student struggles to read with automaticity and frequently stops to sound out words. The student makes more than six errors and rarely self-corrects.

Think Like a Test Maker

If the student is at the instructional or frustration level of reading, independent reading is not the best approach. These students will need supports from the teacher.

Demonstrate knowledge levels of reading comprehension.

Comprehension is the essence of reading. This is when students begin to form images in their minds as they read. They are able to predict what might happen next in a story because they understand what is happening in the story. Students who are in the comprehension stage of reading do not need to decode (sound out) words. They read **fluently** with **prosody**, **automaticity**, and **accuracy**.

Levels of Comprehension

Students have different levels of comprehension at different times. In addition, comprehension questions assess different types of reading comprehension.

- **Literal** – the student can answer questions that can be found in the text.
- **Inferential** – the student can answer questions that are indirectly referenced in the text but not explicitly stated.
- **Evaluative** – the student can move beyond the text and form an opinion about the text based on what is read.

The skills (verbs) at the highest points of the pyramid are apply, evaluate, analyze, and create. When you are faced with a critical thinking problem on the test, visualize this pyramid, and look for answer choices that reflect the higher portions of the pyramid.

Metacognition is thinking about thinking. When students have metacognition, they understand the processes in their minds and can employ a variety of techniques to understand text.

Strategies for boosting **comprehension**, **critical thinking**, and **metacognition** are:

- *Predicting -* Asking students what they think will happen next.
- *Questioning -* Having students ask questions based on what they are reading.
- *Read aloud/think aloud -* Teacher or student reads and stops to think aloud about what the text means.
- *Summarizing -* Asking students to summarize

Quick Tip

A valuable skill used in reading comprehension is **metacognition**. To develop metacognition skills, help students think about the processes they use in their brains as they read through text. We often take these processes for granted. However, when we are aware of what our brain is doing when we read, we can change the process or increase the process to help understand the text.

Use strategies for promoting reading comprehension of imaginative/literary text.

Literary text is fiction that is narrative or tells a story. There are an infinite number of instructional approaches for teaching comprehension of literary texts. The following are a few that you may see on the exam:

Activity	Definition	Example
Jigsaw	A cooperative learning activity in which each student, or groups of students, read and analyze a small piece of information that is part of a much larger piece. They share what they learned with the class.	Teachers arrange students in groups. Each group reads and analyzes a piece of a text. Group members then join with members of other groups, and each student shares and discusses his or her section of the text. As the group shares, the entire text is covered. It is referred to as *Jigsaw* because students complete the puzzle when they share their individual pieces.
Chunking	A reading activity that involves breaking down a difficult text into manageable pieces.	In a science class, students break down a lengthy and complex chapter on genetics by focusing on pieces of the text. The teacher has planned for students to read and analyze the text one paragraph at a time.
Close Reading	Involves the use of evidence-based comprehension strategies embedded in teacher-guided discussions that are planned around repeated readings of a text.	Teacher reads the text aloud and models metacognitive strategies. Students and teacher read the text aloud together and answer guiding questions. In cooperative groups, students reread the text, analyzing the text for different elements.

Think Like a Test Maker

Activity	Definition	Example
Think-Pair-Share	A cooperative learning activity in which students work together to solve a problem or answer a question.	**Think** – The teacher asks a specific question about the text. Students "think" about what they know or have learned about the topic. **Pair** – Students pair up to read and discuss. **Share** - Students share what they've learned in their pairs. Teachers can then expand the "share" into a whole-class discussion.
Reading Response Journals	A writing activity where students use journals to react to what they read by expressing how they feel and asking questions about the text.	After reading a chapter of a book in class, the teacher asks students to use their reading response journals to respond to the story emotionally, make associations between ideas in the text and their own ideas, and record questions they may have about the story.
Evidence-Based Discussion	The teacher sets the expectation that students use evidence in the text to support claims they make during the discussion.	The class is discussing World War II. Students are asking and answering questions. When making claims, students identify support for those claims in the text.
Literature Circles	A small-group, cooperative learning activity where students engage and discuss a piece of literature/ text.	In their cooperative groups, students read and analyze text together. Each student contributes to the learning. There is an administrator who decides when to read and when to stop and discuss. There is a note taker who writes down important information. There are two readers who take turns reading the text based on the administrator's suggestions.
Reciprocal Teaching	An instructional activity in which students become the teacher in small group reading sessions.	After engaging in a close read of a piece of literary text, students facilitate questions exercises and discussion in small groups.

Apply knowledge of evidence-based instructional strategies for developing analysis skills of author's craft and structure.

There are many ways to teach reading comprehension and support metacognition in students as they develop these skills.

Graphic Organizers

A graphic organizer is a visual display of a students' thinking process as they work through text. There are many types of graphic organizers that serve different purposes. The following are a few of the main graphic organizers students use for literary text.

- **Venn Diagram** – Compares and contrasts story elements, characters, setting, etc.
- **Story map** – Organizes elements of the story including characters, plot, sequence, and major events.

- **Timeline** – organizes events in the story chronologically.
- **Sequence map** – Sequences the story's main events

Close reading of imaginative/literary text

Close reading is an instructional approach to reading complex text where students may or may not have extensive prior or background knowledge. The teacher and students read the text multiple times using different approaches and different perspectives. Below is a typical sequence of close reading:

1. The teacher reads aloud the text to students while students follow along.

2. The teacher rereads important parts of the text and discusses with students the author's purpose, characterization, sequence, and other story elements.

3. Then students read the story aloud using automaticity and prosody.

Promoting higher order thinking

Comprehension is a higher order skill. While they read, students must create pictures in their minds, predict, summarize, question, and analyze. These methods are considered critical thinking skills. Teachers must help students develop these skills by:

- Asking students higher-order questions
- Using wait time to allow student time to process and think about the question
- Increasing question complexity incrementally as students gain understanding
- Engaging in text-based discussions
- Requiring students use evidence to support claims

Major Theorists in Second Language Acquisition

Theorist	Theory
Krashen	5 main hypotheses of second language acquisition 1. Acquisition-learning hypothesis 2. Monitor Hypothesis 3. Input Hypothesis 4. Affective Filter hypothesis 5. Natural Order Hypothesis
Cummins	**BICS** (basic interpersonal communication skills) **CALP** (cognitive academic language proficiency). CALP is the basis for ELLs' ability to cope with the academic demands placed on them in the various subjects.
Chomsky	Transformational Gramma Universal Grammar

Other Important policies

Texas Specific

Language Proficiency Assessment Committee (LPAC) – This is a committee that evaluates the proficiency of ELLs. The committee uses data, screening, and other measures to determine where students should be placed.

Admission, Review and Dismissal (ARD) – This group decides whether the student is admitted to an ESL program and when it's time, dismissed.

Students who are ELL and who have disabilities

When a student with a disability is, or might be identified as an emergent bilingual (EB)/English learner (EL), the student's admission, review, and dismissal (ARD) committee must work in conjunction with the language proficiency assessment committee (LPAC) to ensure appropriate identification and reclassification procedures and to determine recommended participation in the required bilingual education or English as a second language (ESL) program.

This page intentionally left blank.

Bibliography

Artiles, A. & Klingner, J. (2006). Forging a knowledge base on English language learners with special needs: Theoretical, population, and technical issues. Teachers College Record, 108(11) 2187-2194.

Cherry, K. (2020). How does implicit bias affect behavior. *Very Well Mind*. Retrieved from https://www.verywellmind.com/implicit-bias-overview-4178401

ETS TEOFL (2015) *Learn these 4 word stress rules to improve your pronunciation.* Retrieved from https://www.toeflgoanywhere.org/learn-these-4-word-stress-rules-improve-your-pronunciation

Glossary of Education Reform (2015). *Test Bias.* Retrieved from https://www.edglossary.org/test-bias/

Glossary of Education Reform (2019). Student-centered learning. Retrieved from https://www.edglossary.org/student-centered-learning/

Gordillo, W., (2015). Top 10 trends in special education. Retrieved from\ https://www.scilearn.com/blog/2015-special-education-trends

Heggerty, Ed.D., M. (2003). *Phonemic Awareness: The Skills They Need to Help Them Succeed!* https://wps.prenhall.com/chet_nes_v2bridgedemo_1/185/47611/12188671.cw/content/index.html

Hurst, S. (2014). *What's the difference between RTI and MTSS?* Reading Horizons. Retrieved from https://www.readinghorizons.com/blog/what-is-the-difference-between-rti-and-mtss

Krashen, S. (1981). Second Language Acquisition and Second Language Learning. Oxford: Pergamon Press.

Rivera et al. (2006). Research-Based Recommendations for Instruction and Academic Interventions. Practical Guidelines for the Education of English Language Learners. Book 1 of 3. Center on Instruction.

Rossi-Landi, Ferruccio (1973). *Ideologies of Linguistic Relativity*. The Hague: Mouton.

The U.S. Department of Education (2015). Disabilities discrimination: Overview of the laws. Office for Civil Rights. Retrieved from https://www2.ed.gov/about/offices/list/ocr/disabilityoverview.html

The U.S. Department of Education (2019). Family Education Rights and Privacy Act. Retrieved from https://www2.ed.gov/policy/gen/guid/fpco/ferpa/index.html

The U.S. Department of Education (2021). Every Student Succeeds Act (ESSA). Retrieved from https://www.ed.gov/essa

The U.S. Department of Education (2021). No Child Left Behind (NCLB). Retrieved from https://www.ed.gov/nclb

Wagner, R. K., & Torgesen, J. K. (1987). The nature of phonological processing and its causal role in the acquisition of reading skills. *Psychological Bulletin, 101*, 192-212.

Wall, Joan (1989). *International phonetic alphabet for singers: A manual for English and foreign language diction*. Pst.

Weselby, C. (2014). What is differentiated instruction? Examples of how to differentiate instruction in the classroom. Retrieved from https://education.cu-portland.edu/blog/classroom-resources/examples-of-differentiated-instruction/

Whitehurst, G., & Lonigan, C. (1998). Child Development and Emergent Literacy. *Child Development, 69*(3), 848-872. doi:10.2307/1132208

WIDA (2012). The English language development standards. Retrieved from https://wida.wisc.edu/sites/default/files/resource/2012-ELD-Standards.pdf